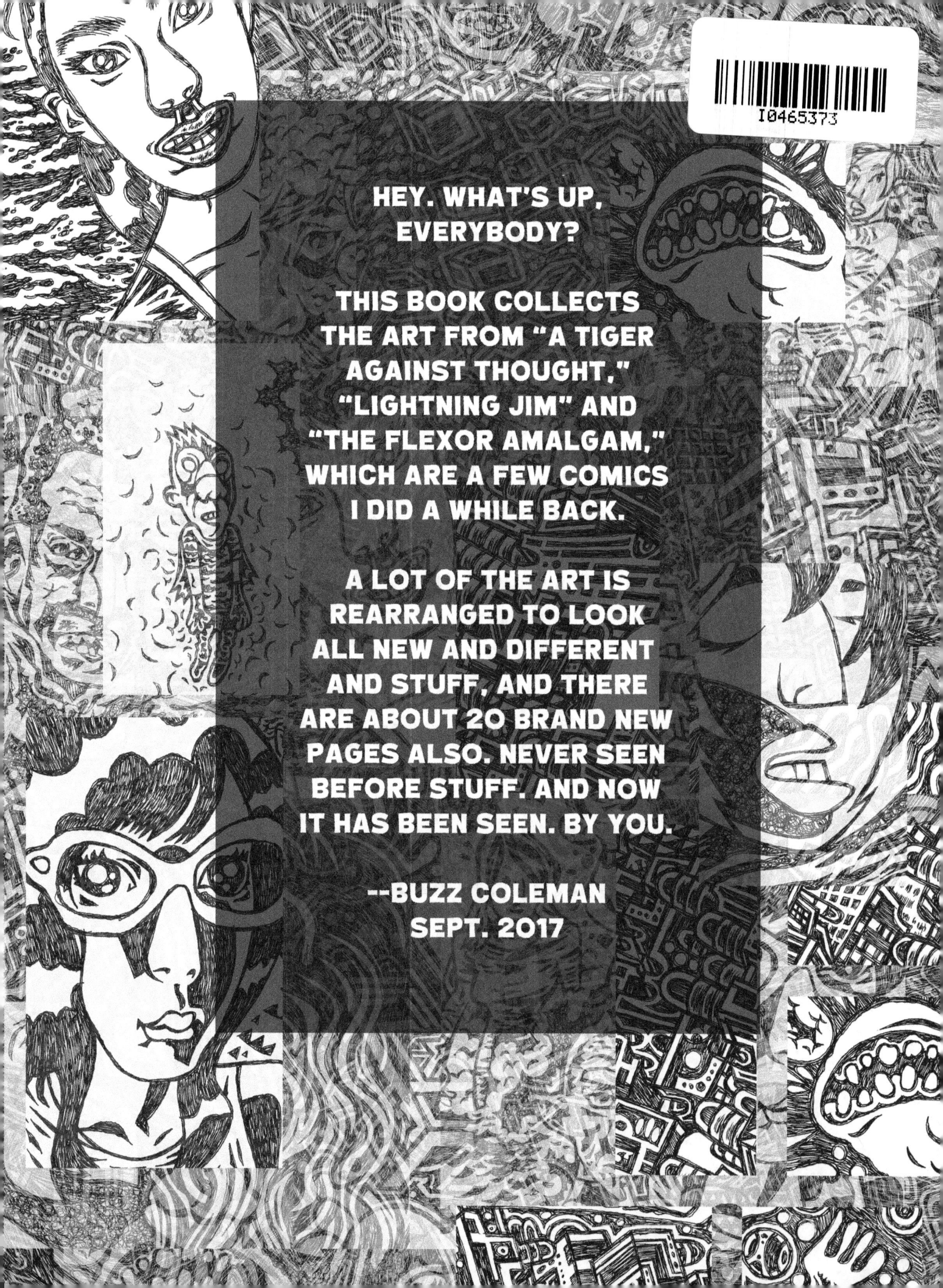

HEY. WHAT'S UP, EVERYBODY?

THIS BOOK COLLECTS THE ART FROM "A TIGER AGAINST THOUGHT," "LIGHTNING JIM" AND "THE FLEXOR AMALGAM," WHICH ARE A FEW COMICS I DID A WHILE BACK.

A LOT OF THE ART IS REARRANGED TO LOOK ALL NEW AND DIFFERENT AND STUFF, AND THERE ARE ABOUT 20 BRAND NEW PAGES ALSO. NEVER SEEN BEFORE STUFF. AND NOW IT HAS BEEN SEEN. BY YOU.

--BUZZ COLEMAN
SEPT. 2017

DRUID FLUID PRESENTS

THE SCRATCHY EYE
SOME DRAWINGS
BY BUZZ COLEMAN

THIS BOOK IS DEDICATED TO
ALL THE POWER RINGS, BUT
THE EMERALD ONE MOST OF ALL.
IT WILL ALWAYS BE THE CLOSEST
TO MY SOFTEST HEART.

THANKS FOR ALL THE JOURNEYS!
A TEAR IN MY EYE AND A FIST IN THE AIR!!!

CHECK OUT MORE ART AND COMICS AT:

THEDRUIDFLUIDCOMIC.BLOGSPOT.JP

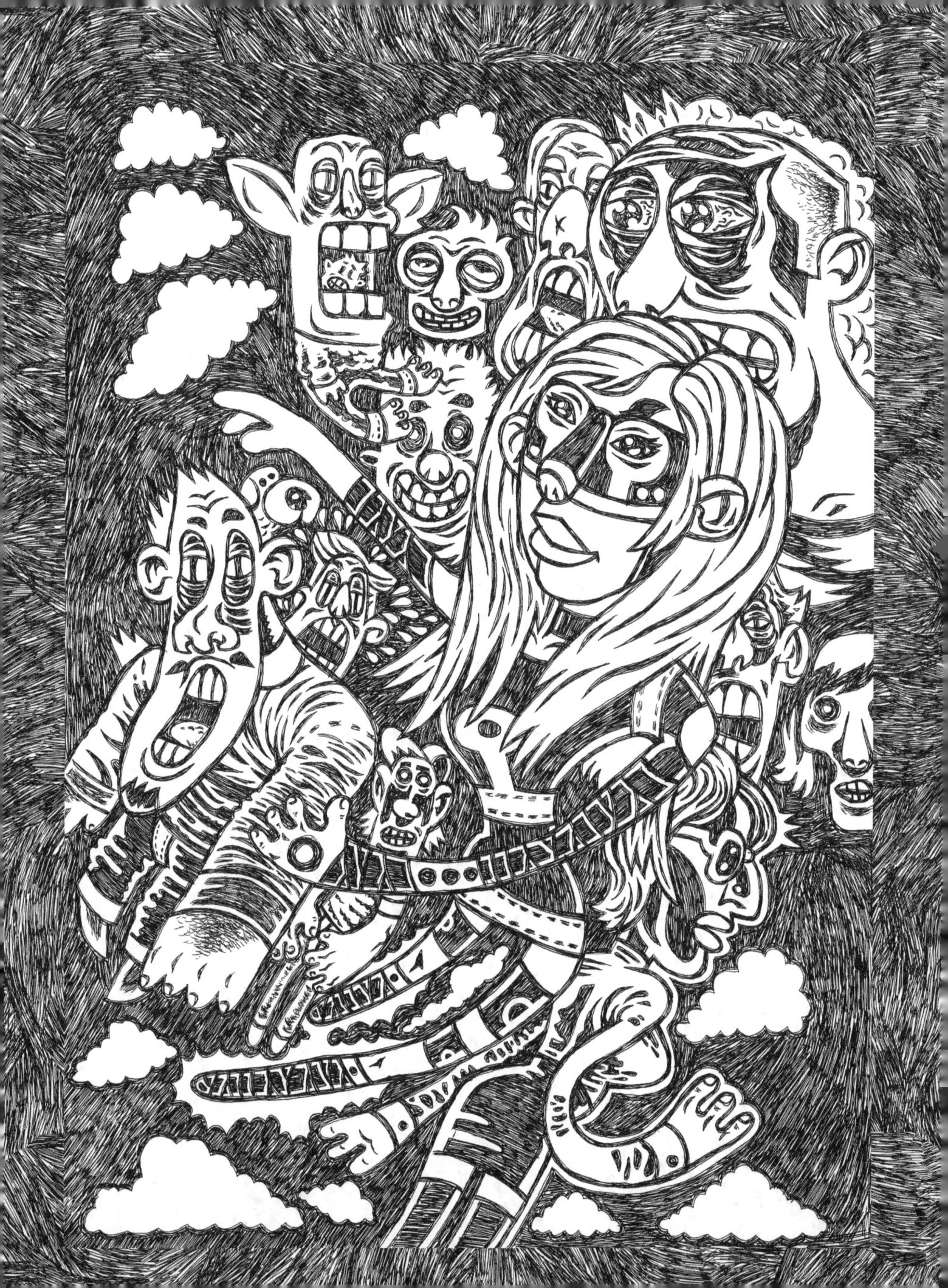

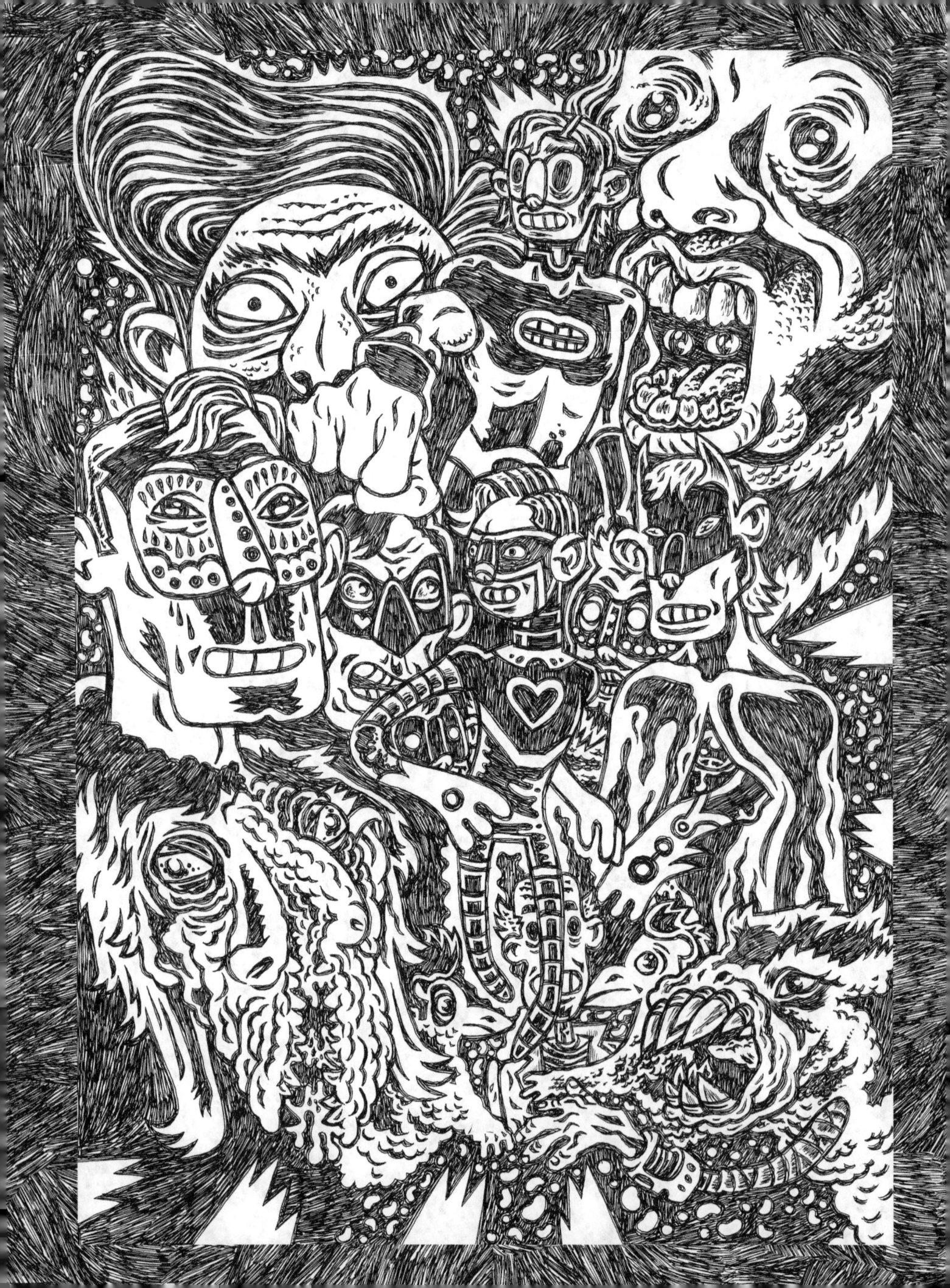

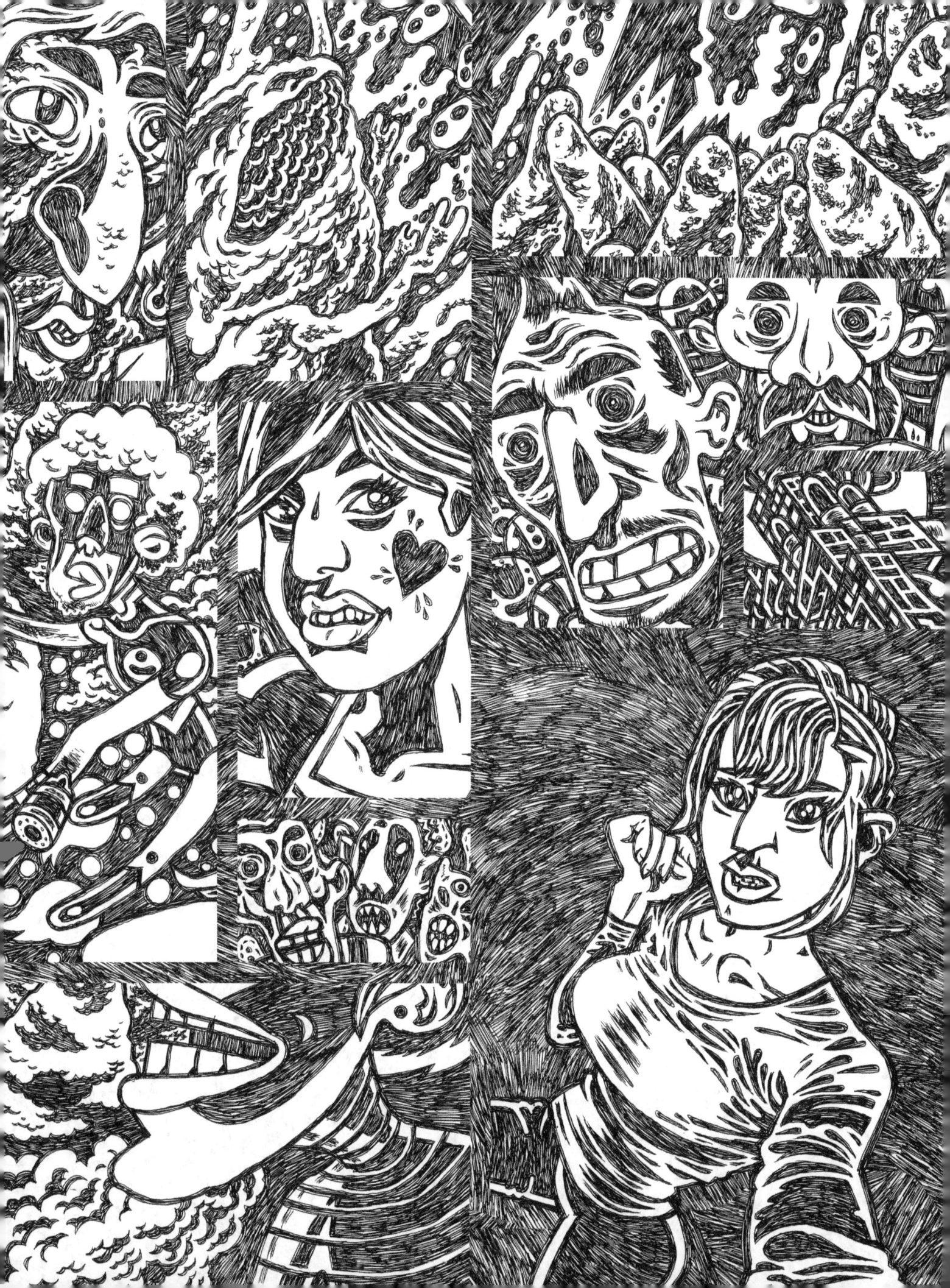

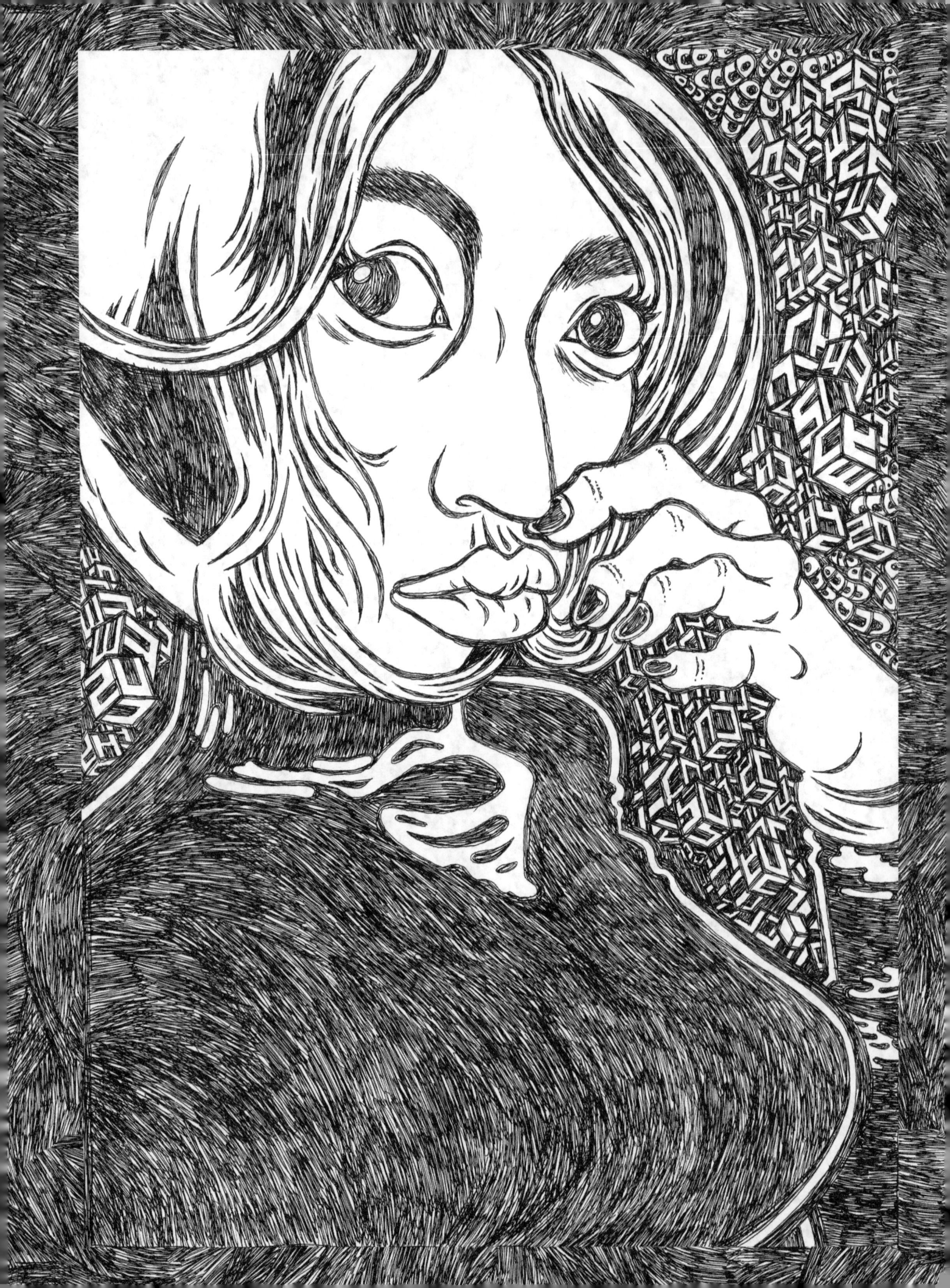

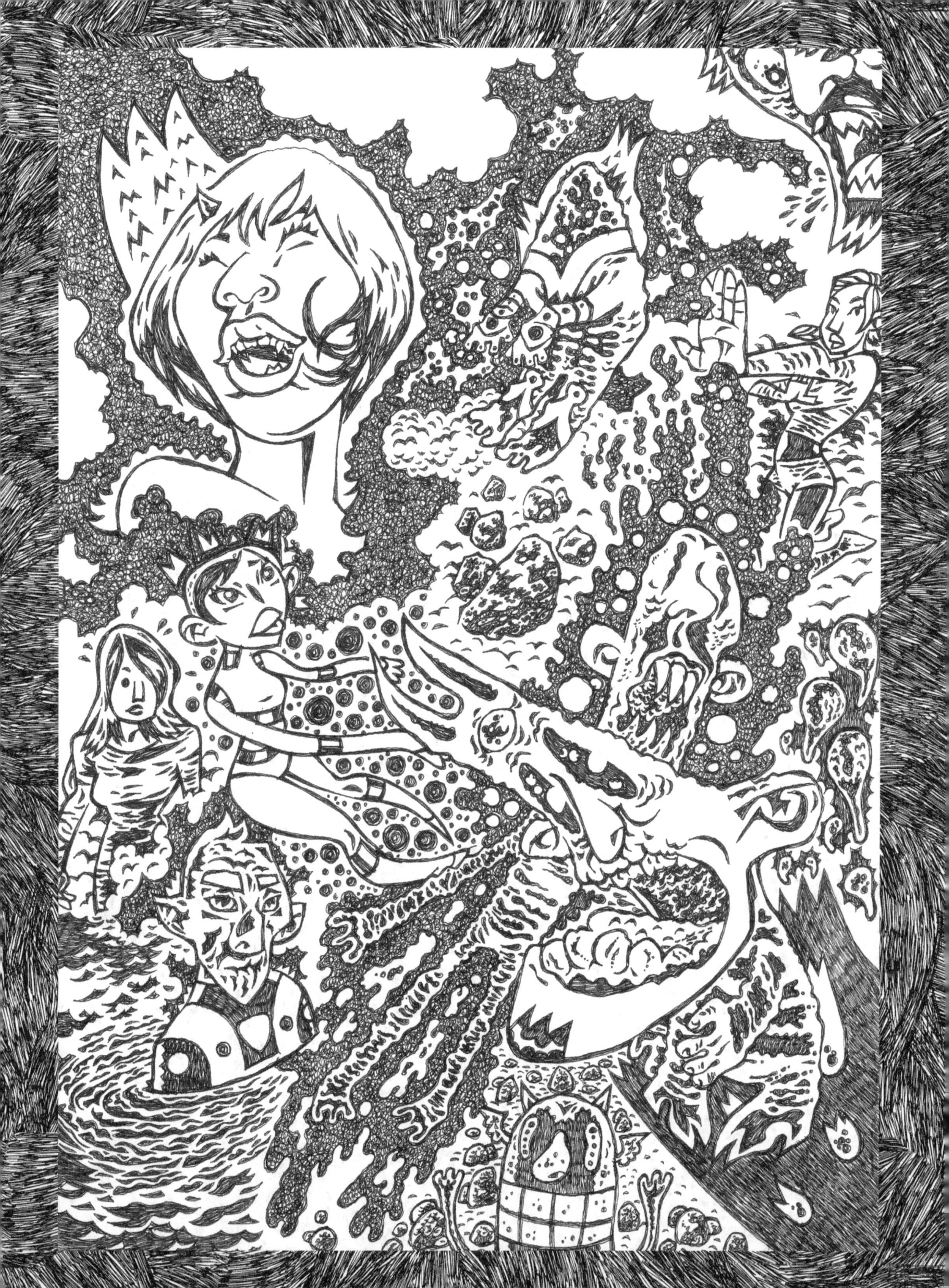

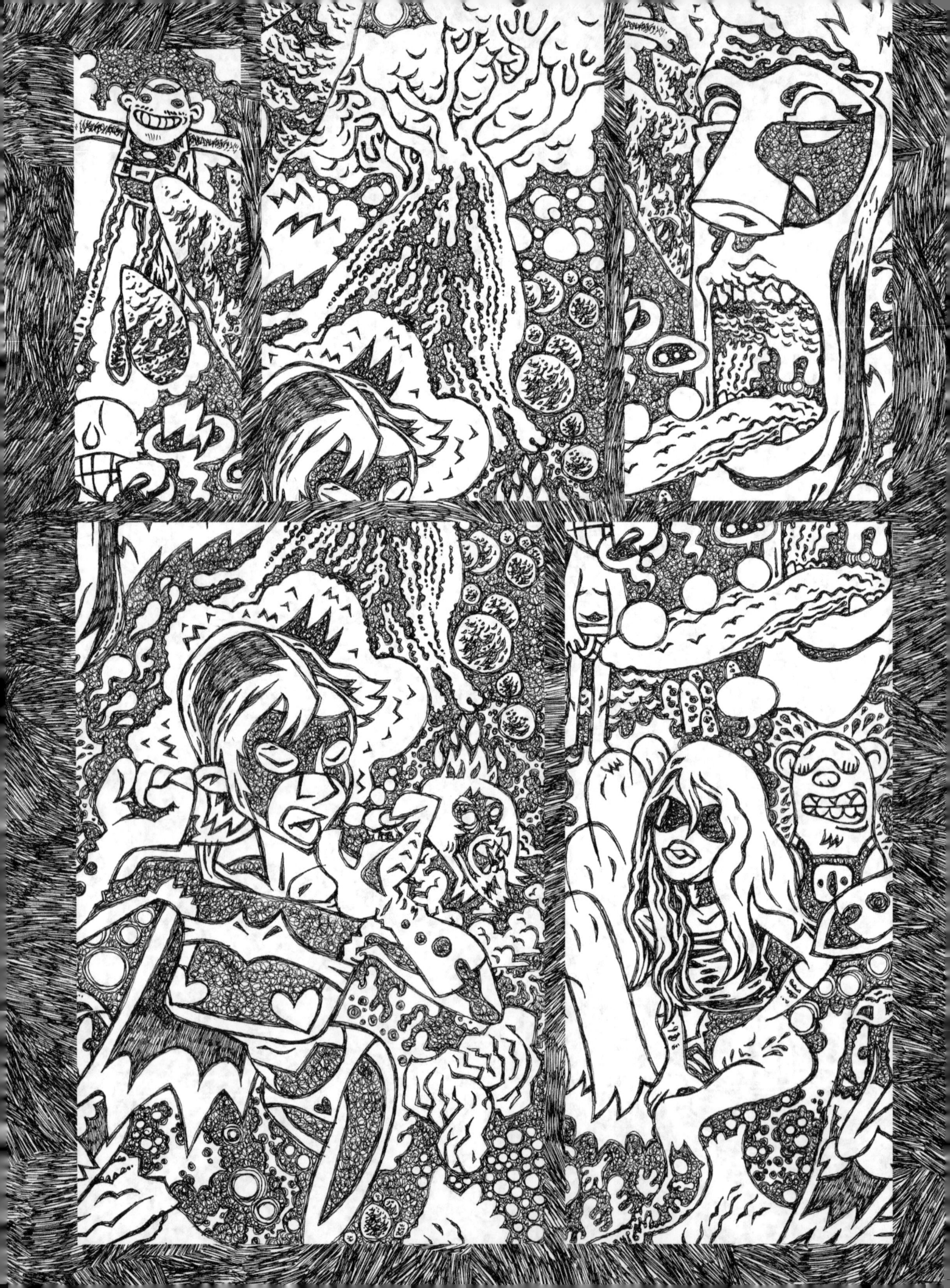

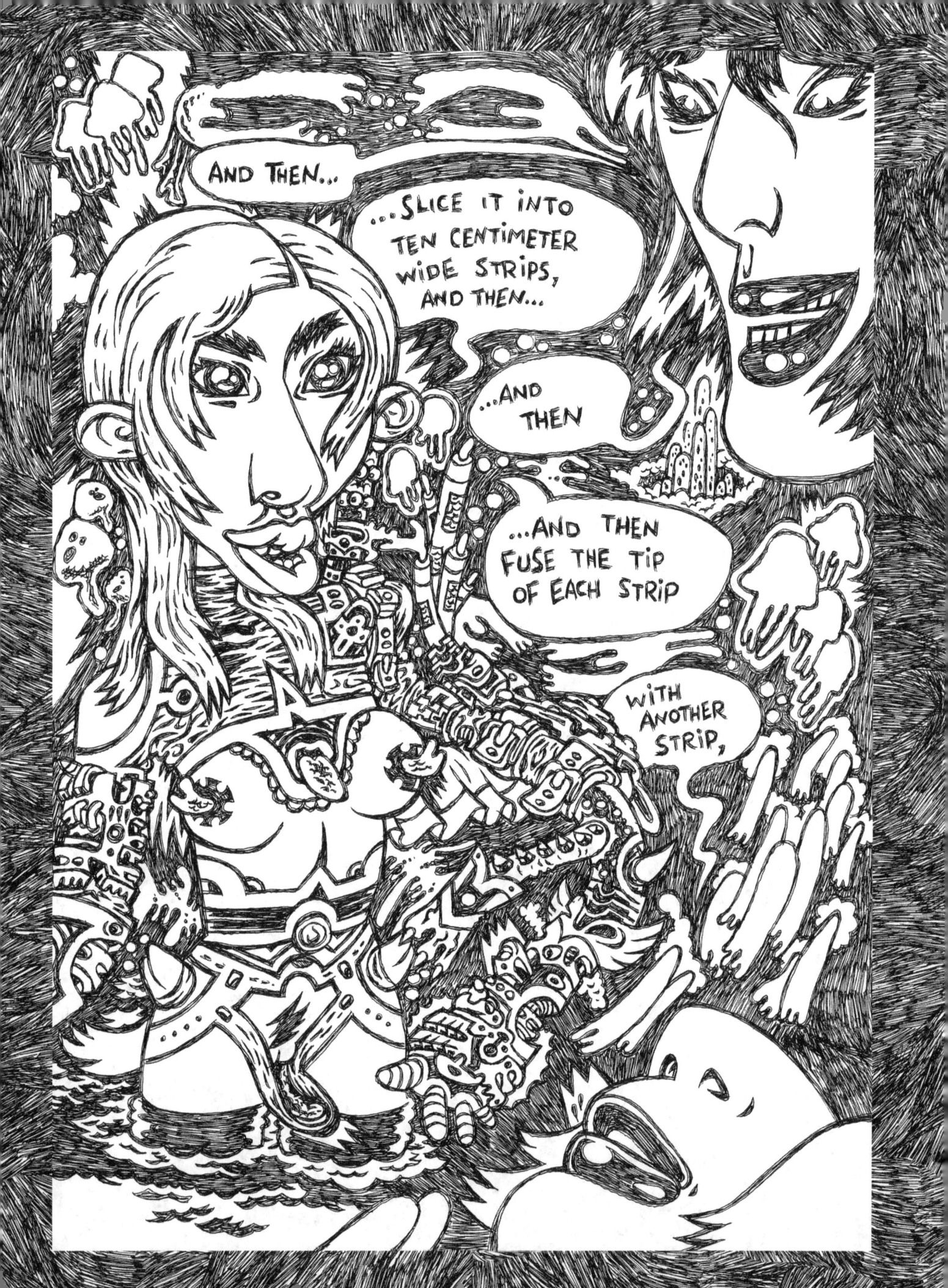

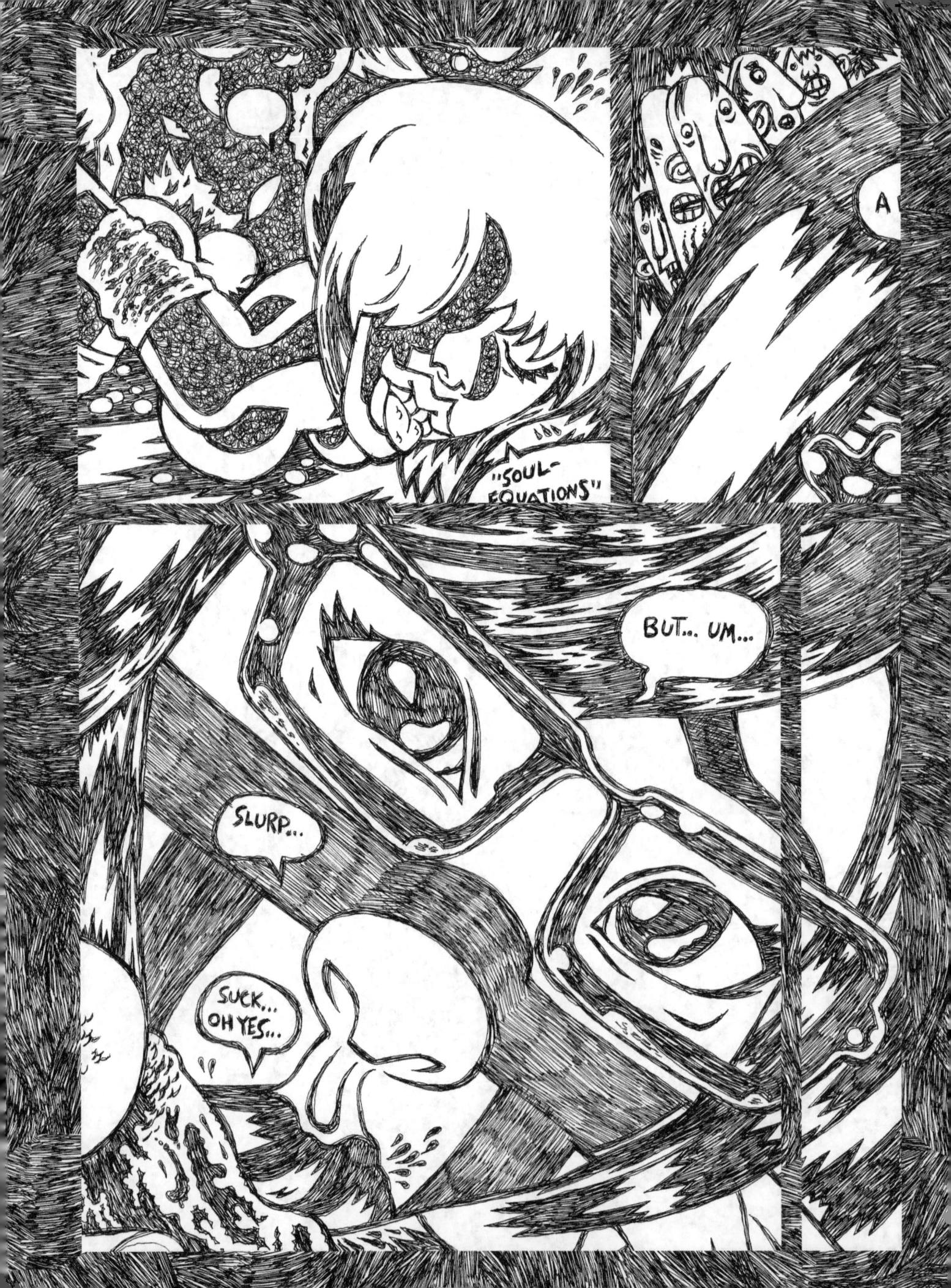

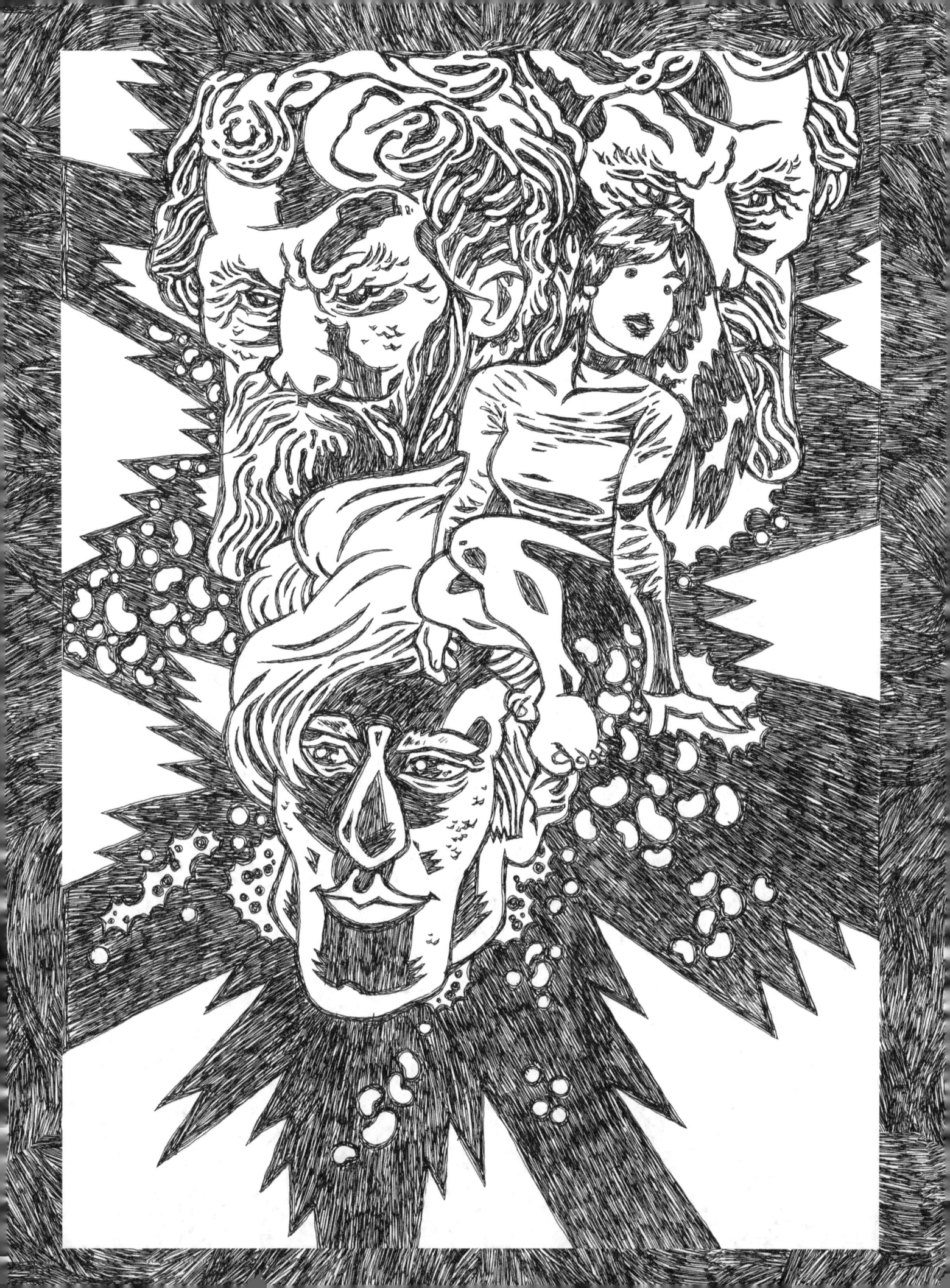

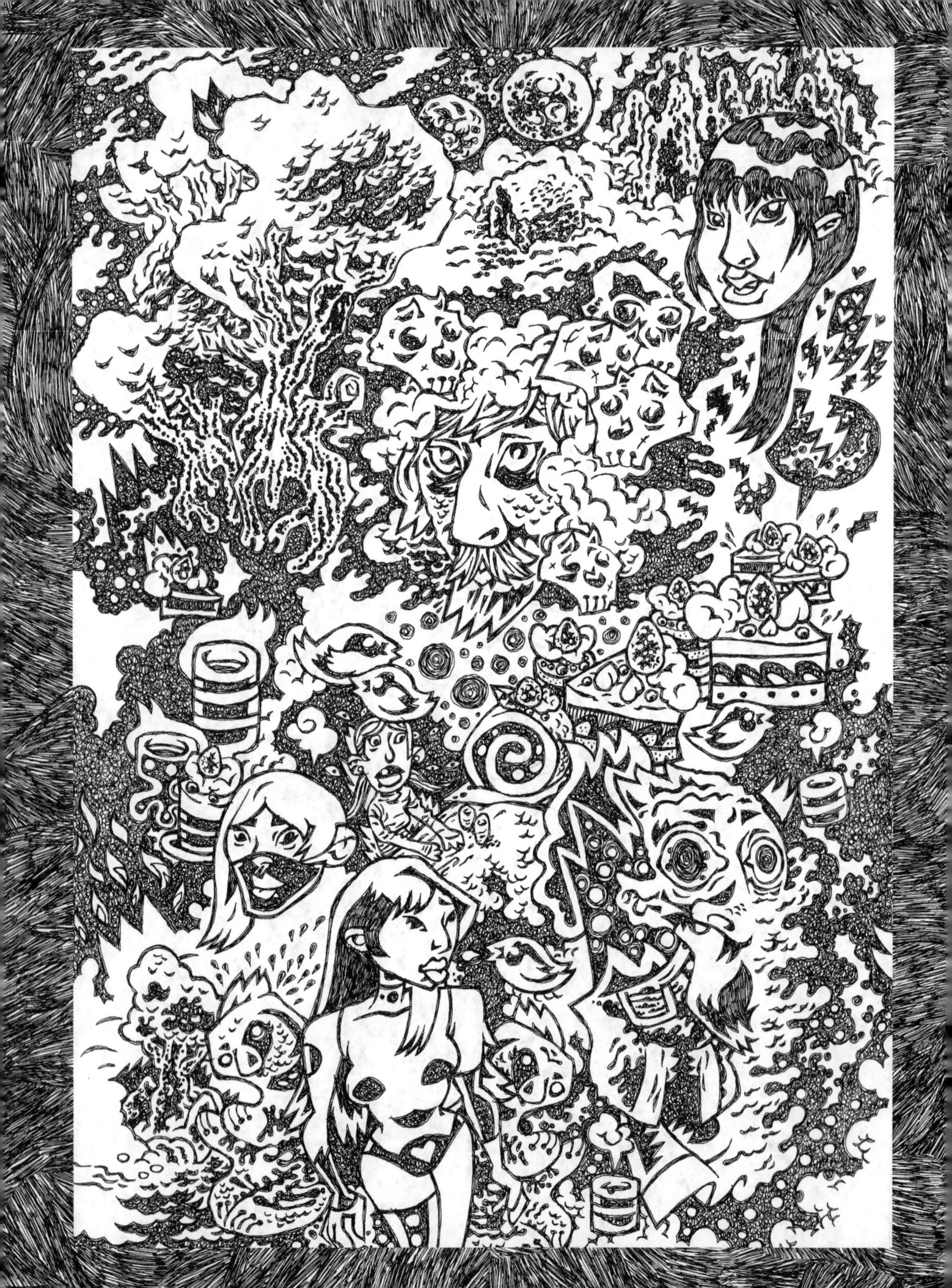

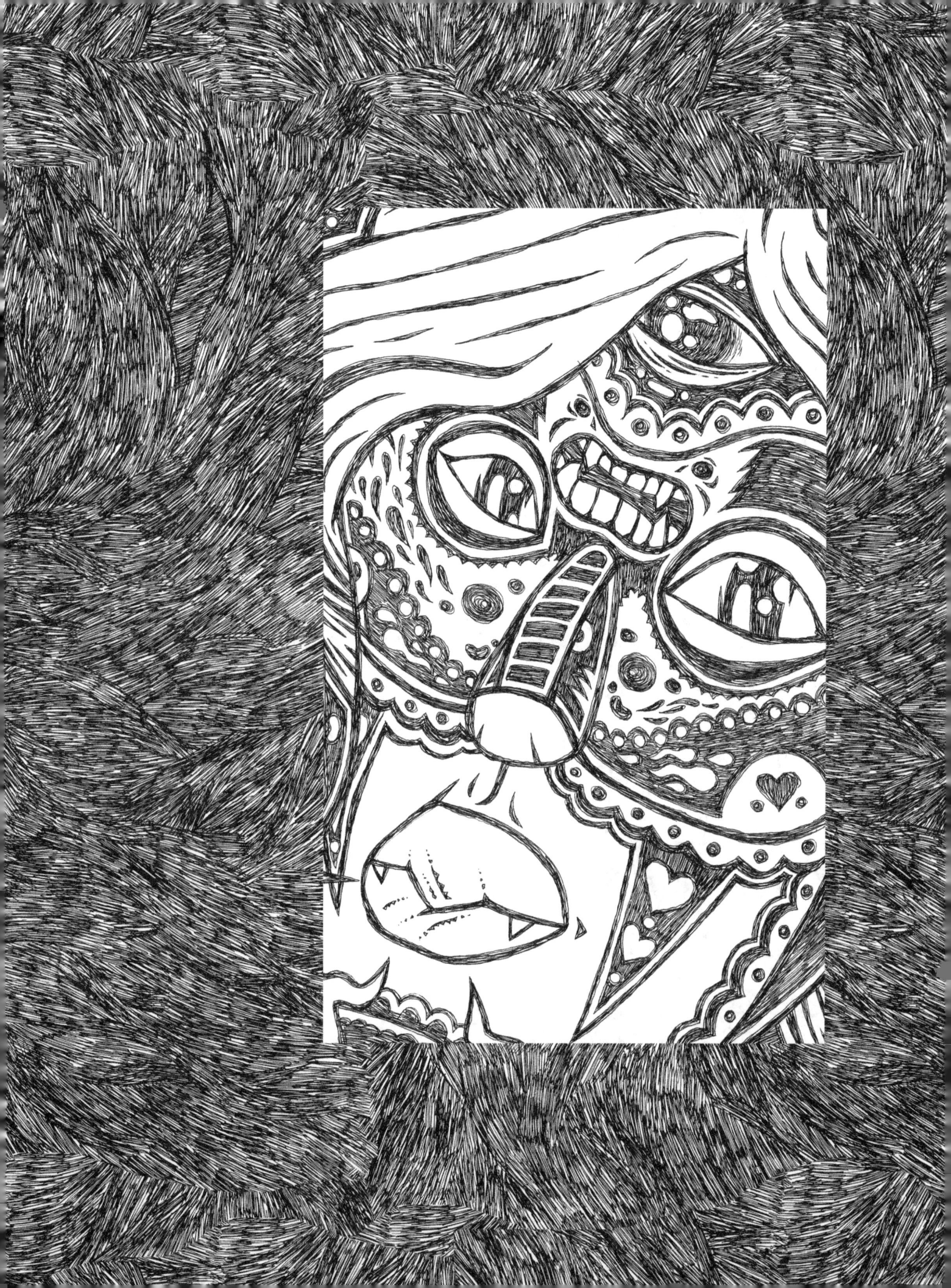

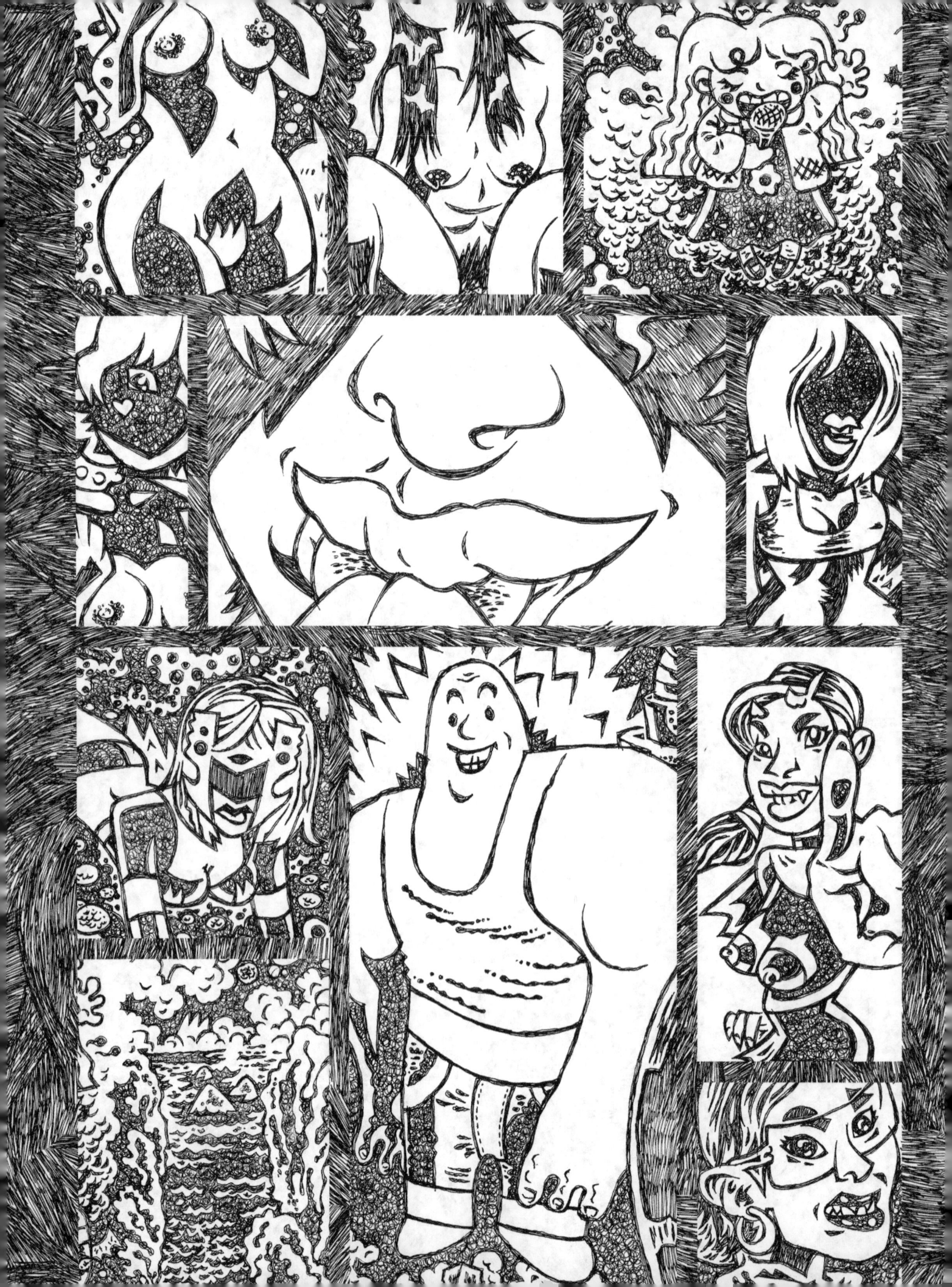

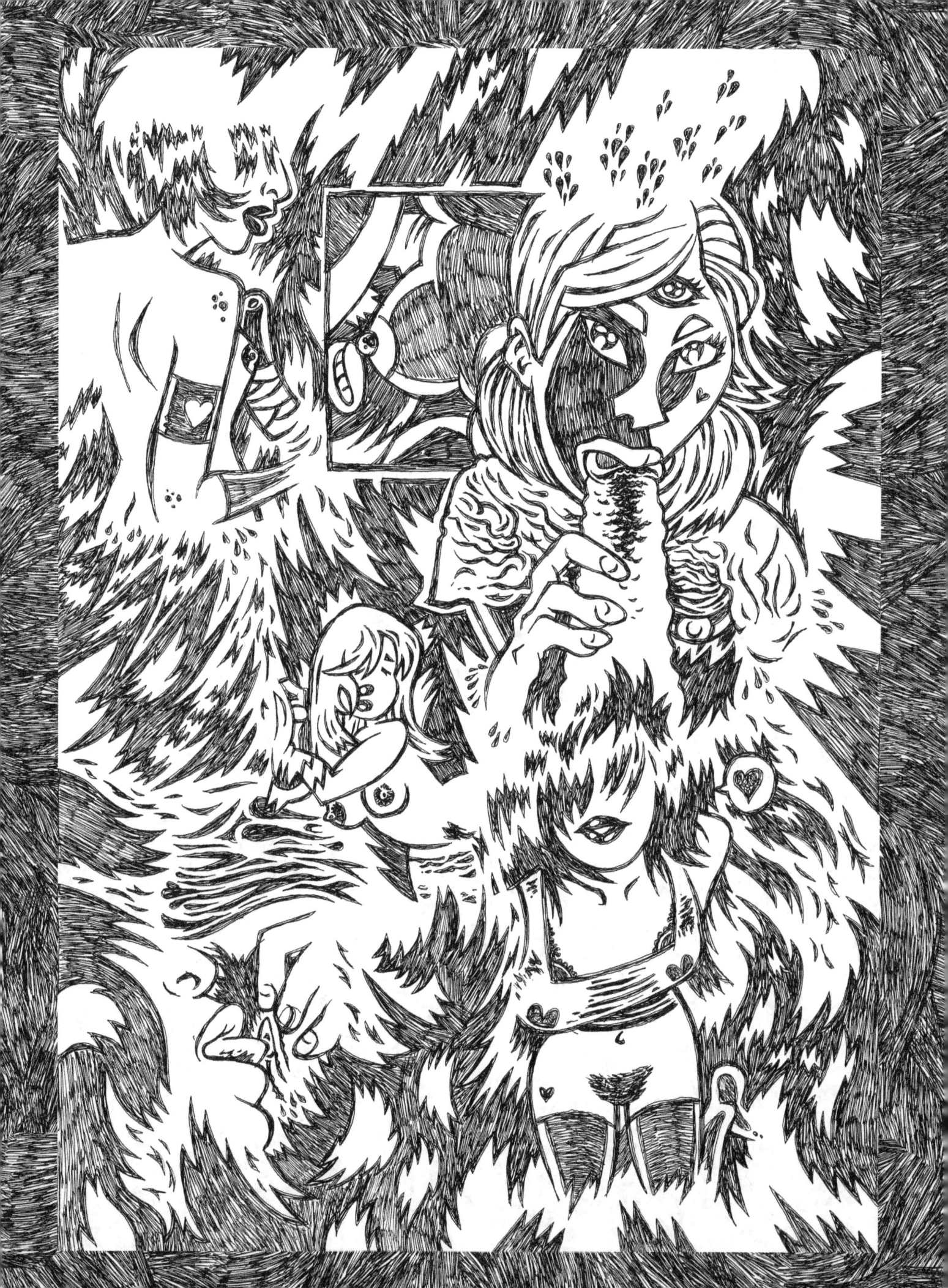

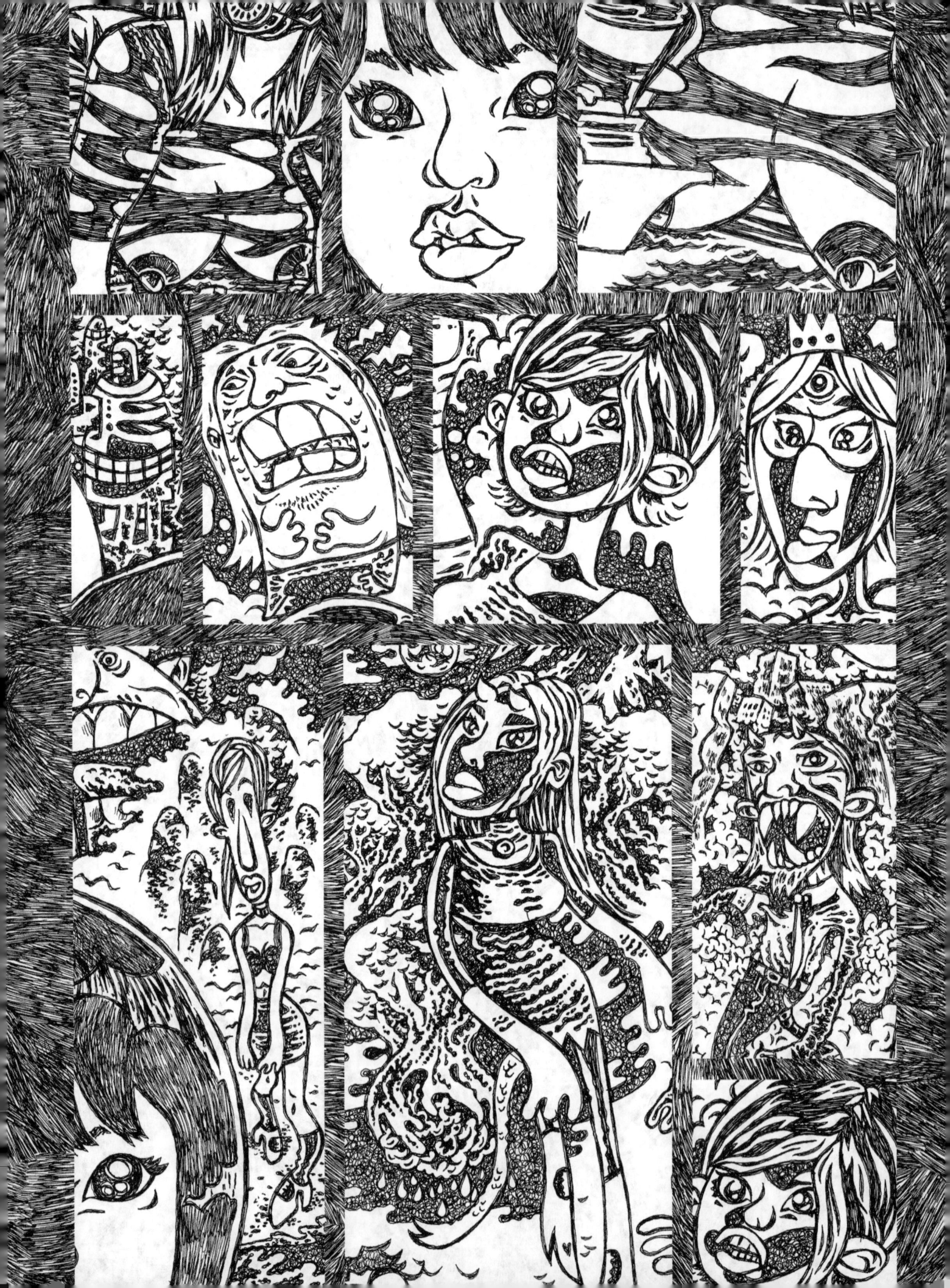

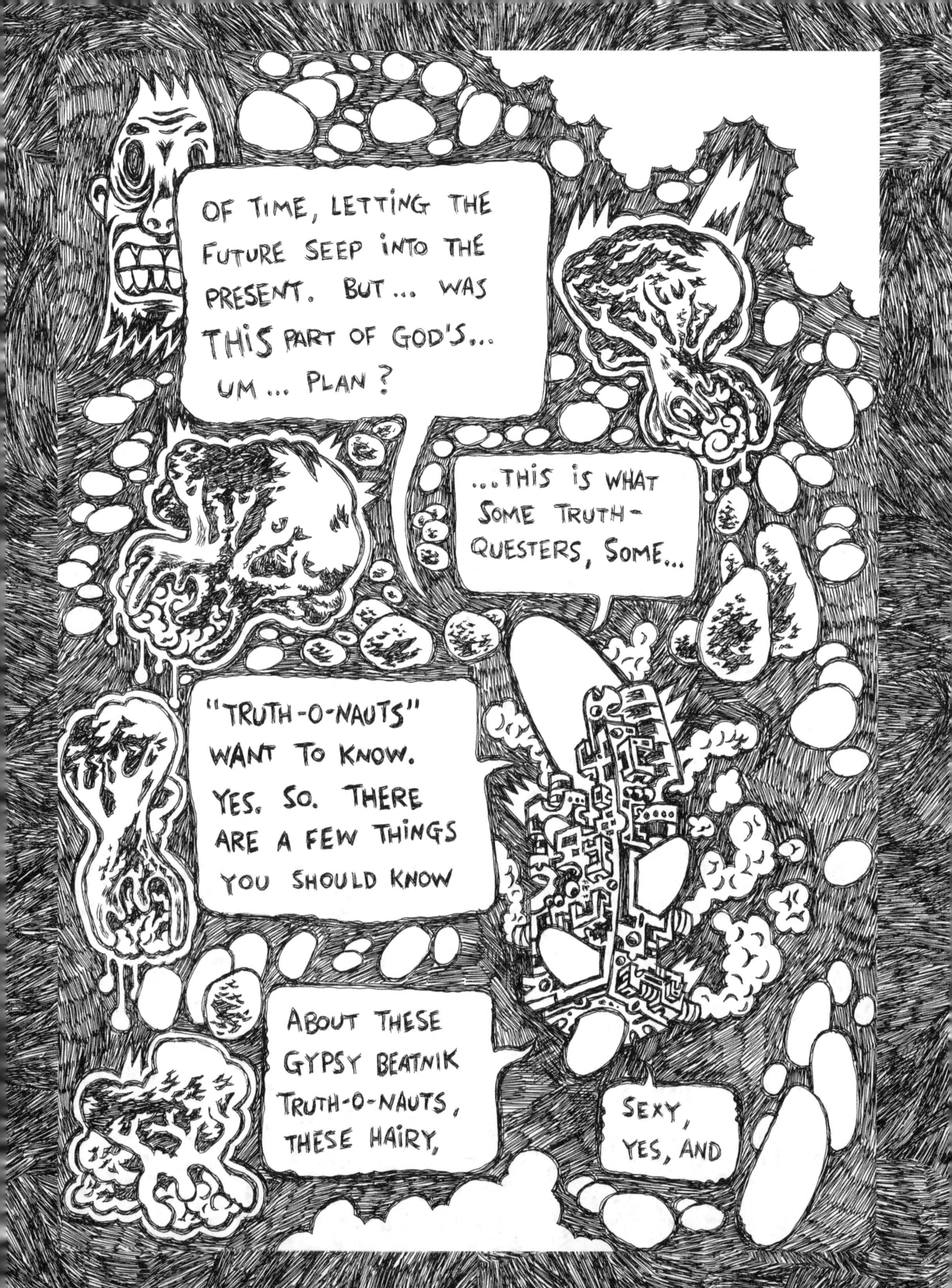

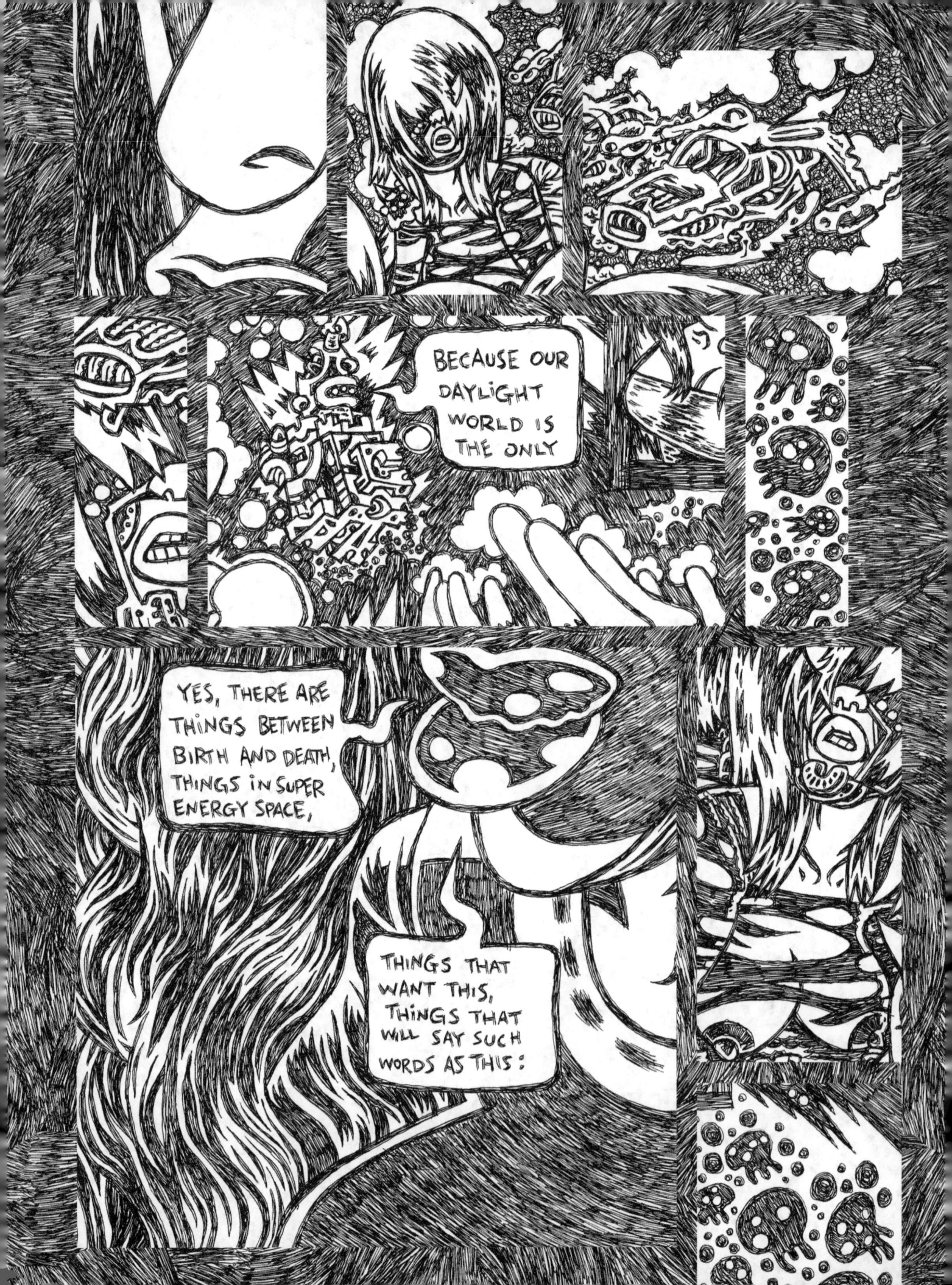

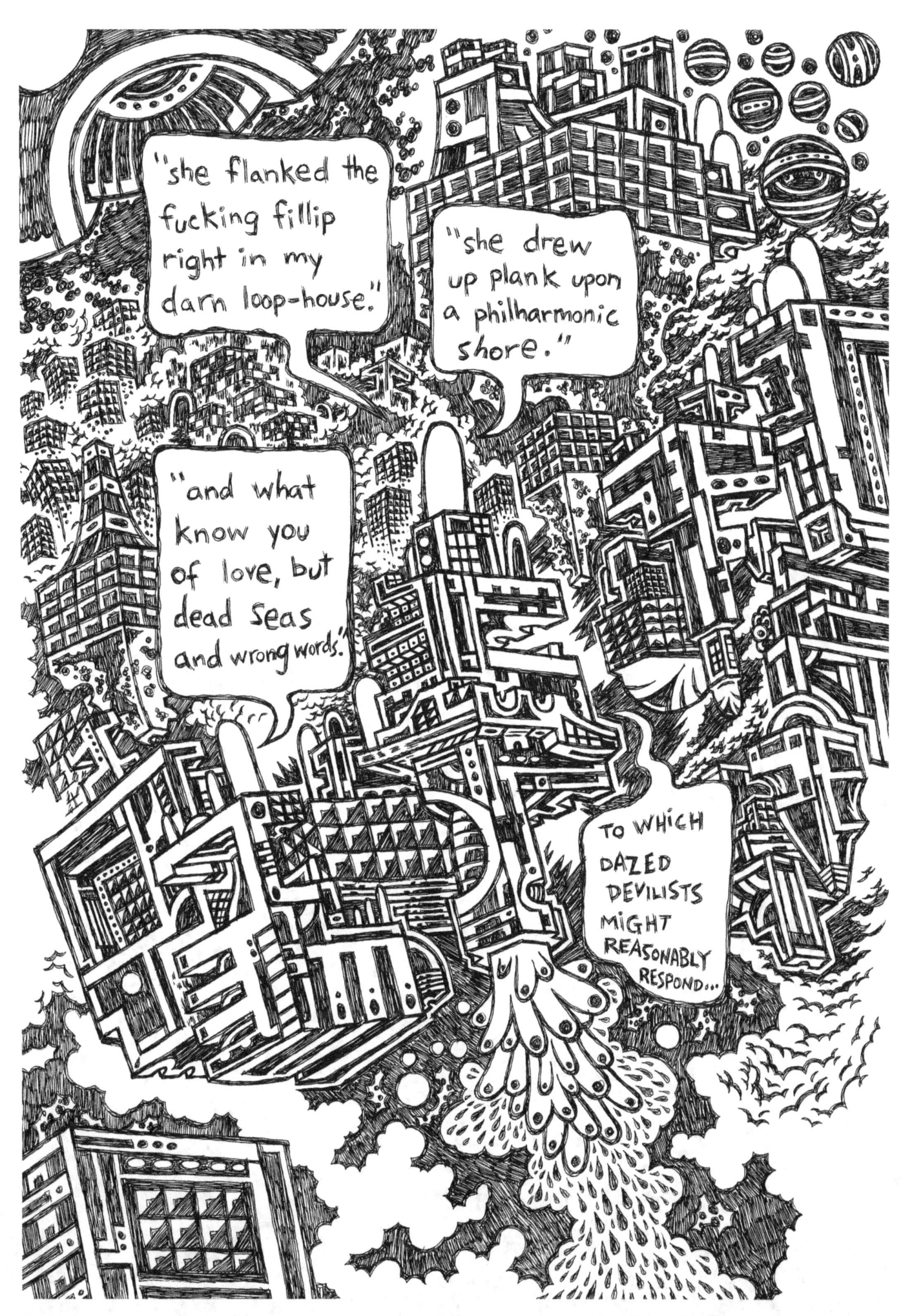

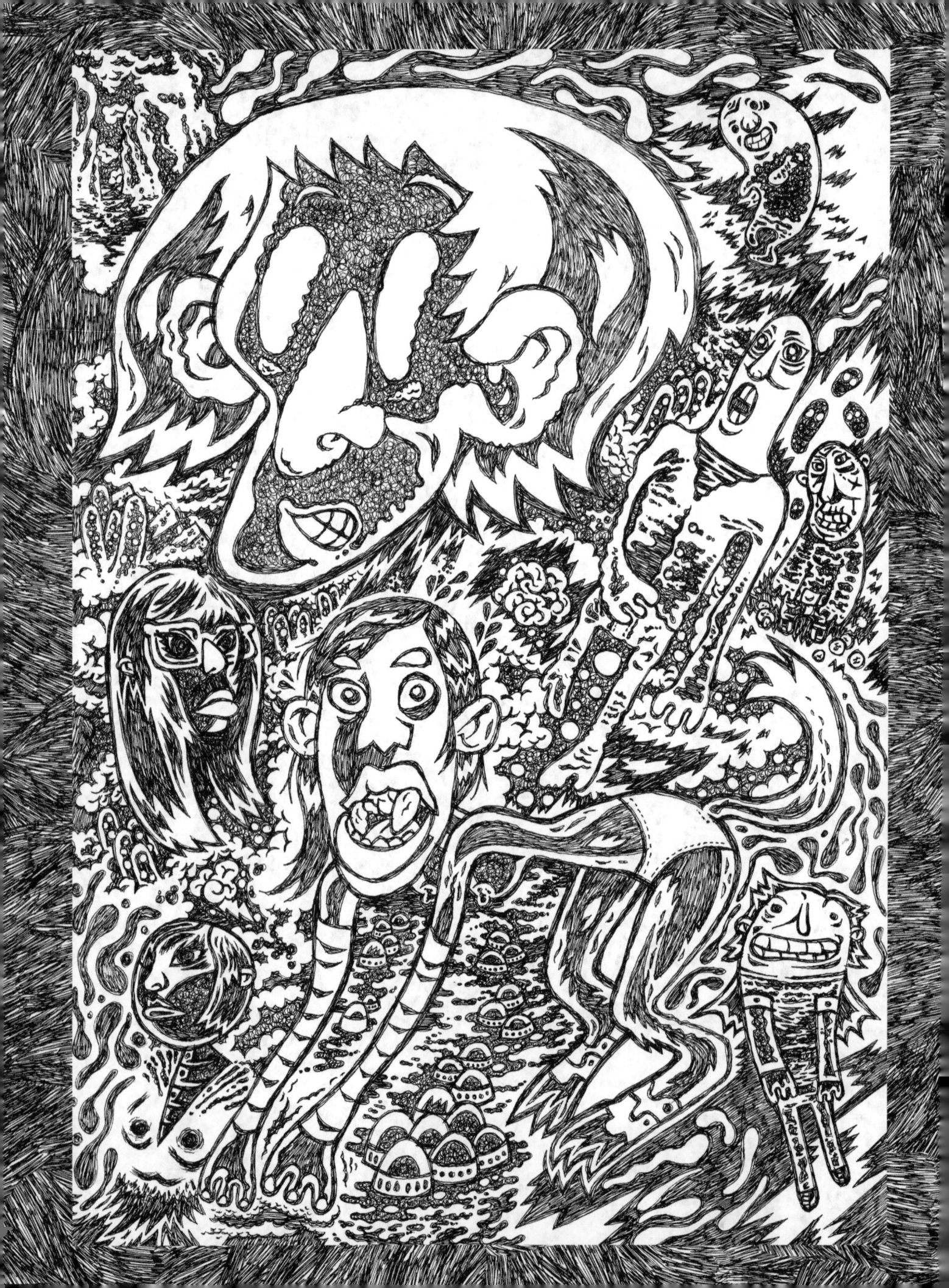

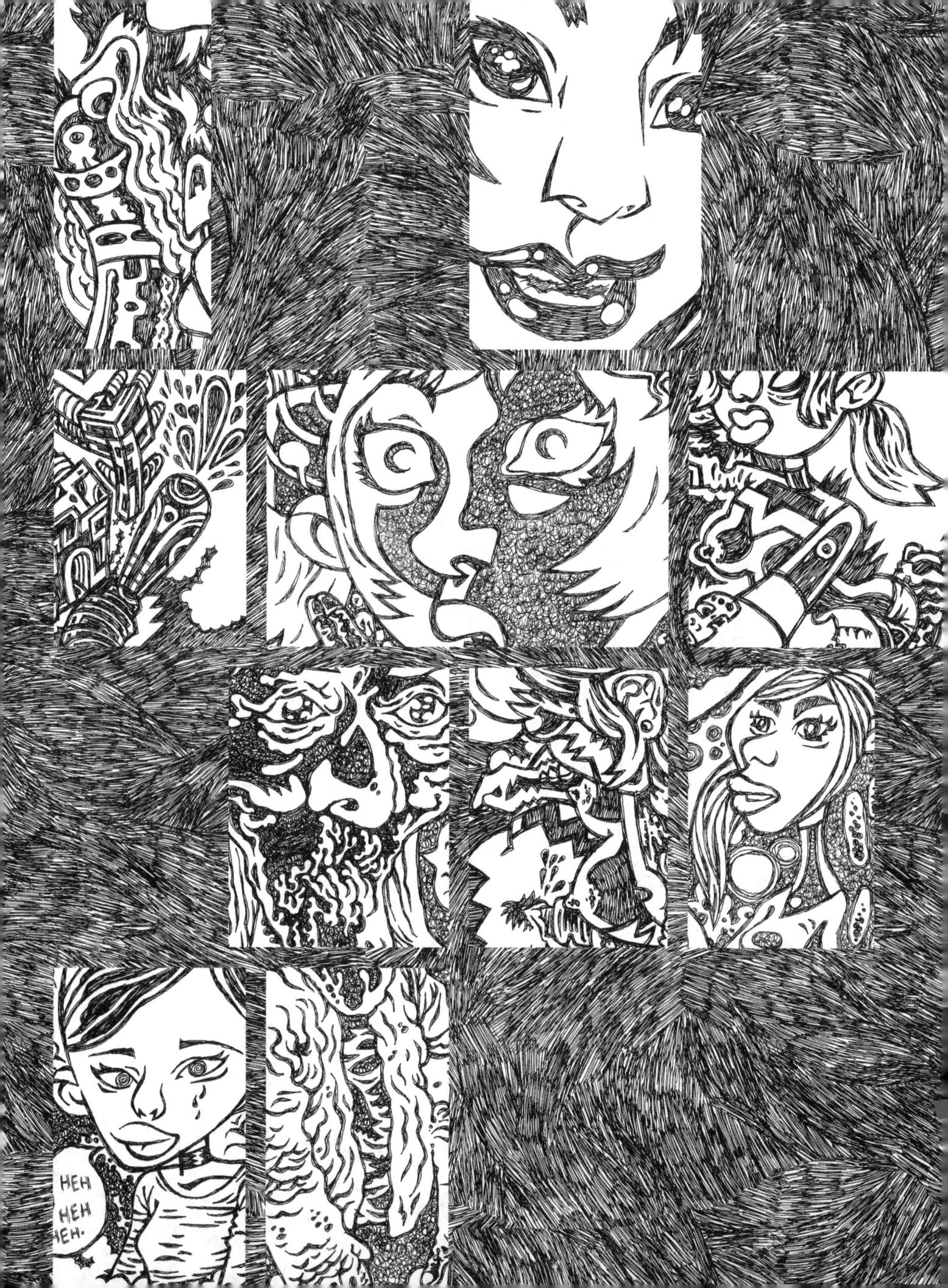

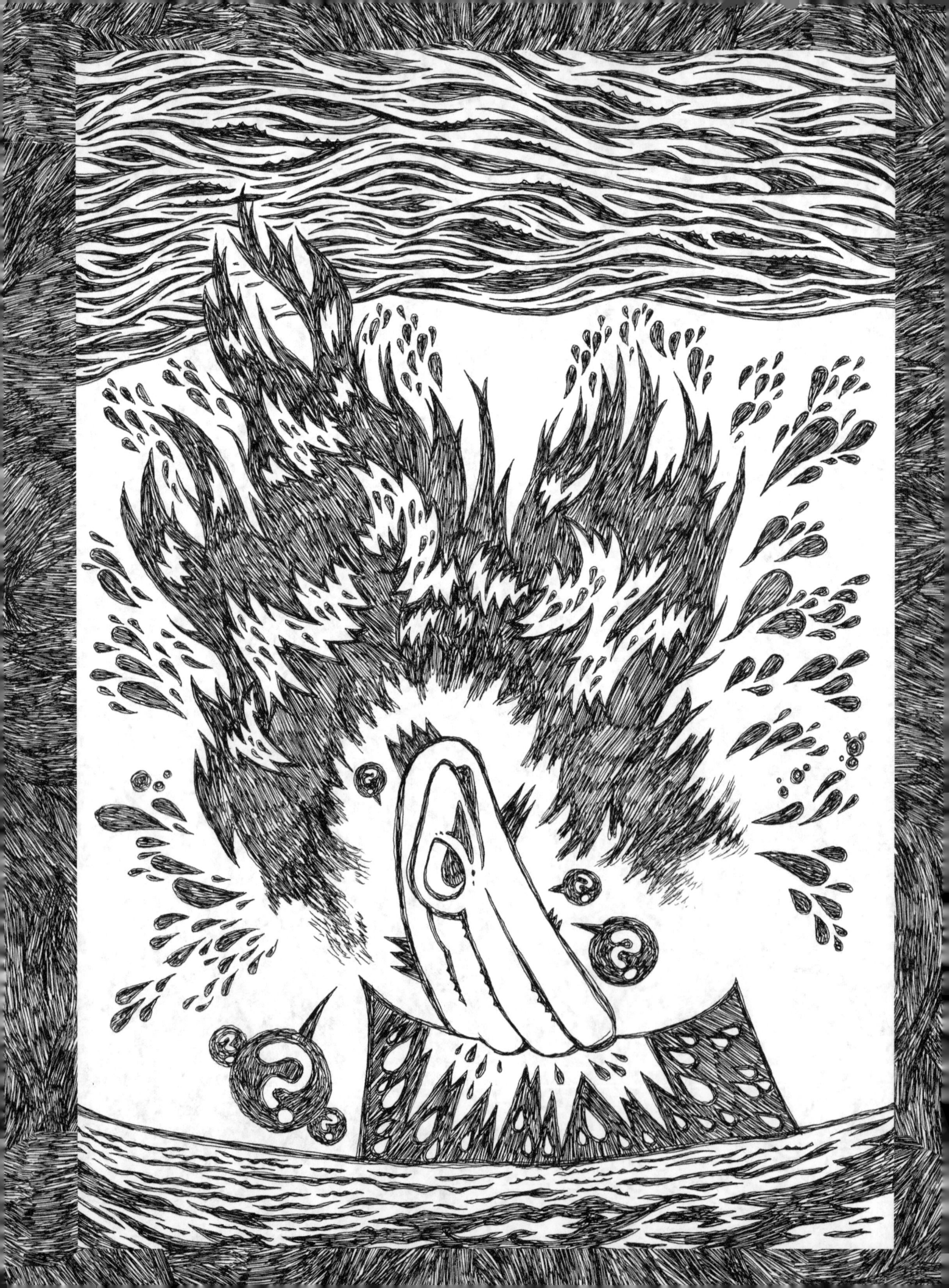

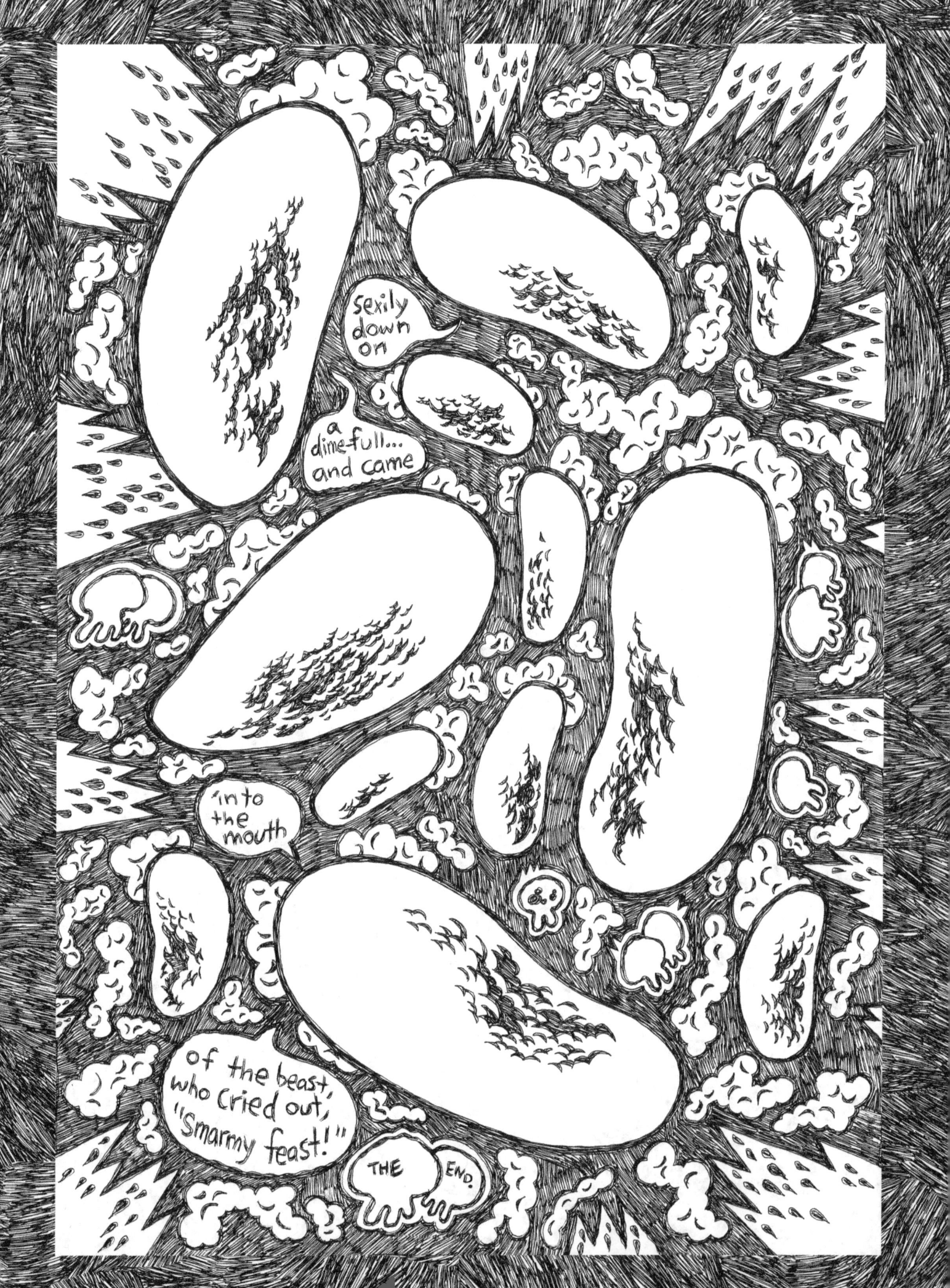

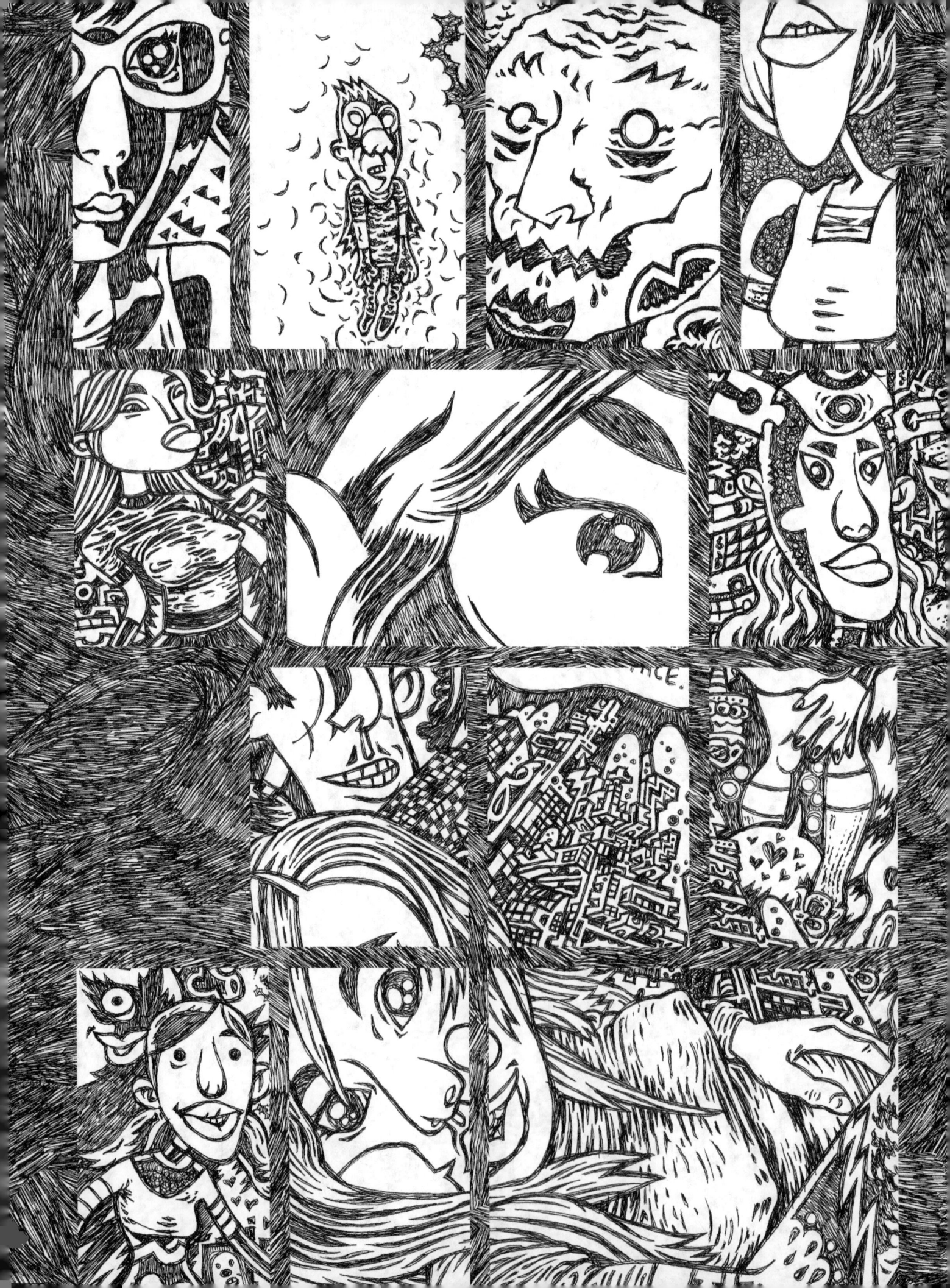

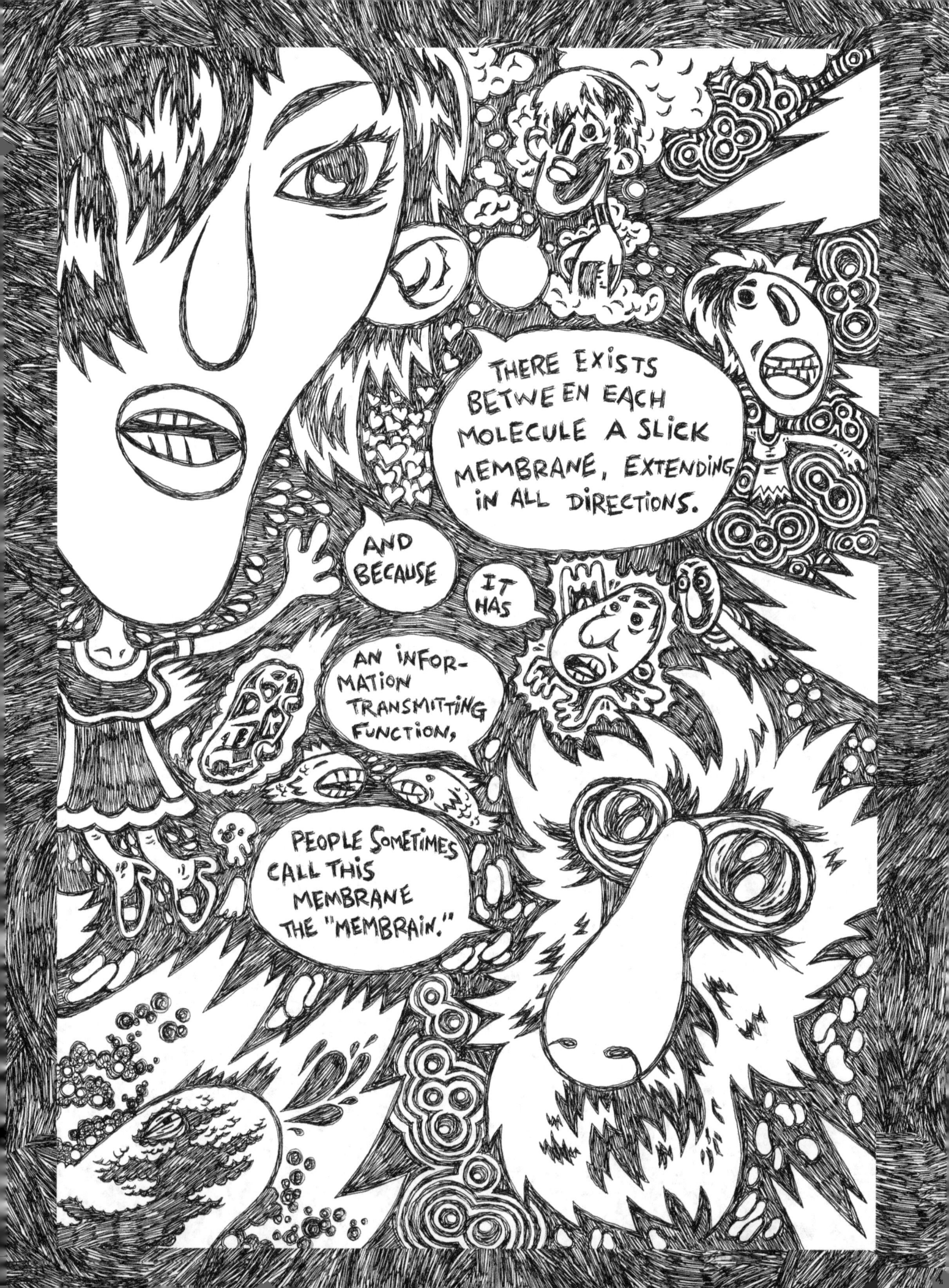

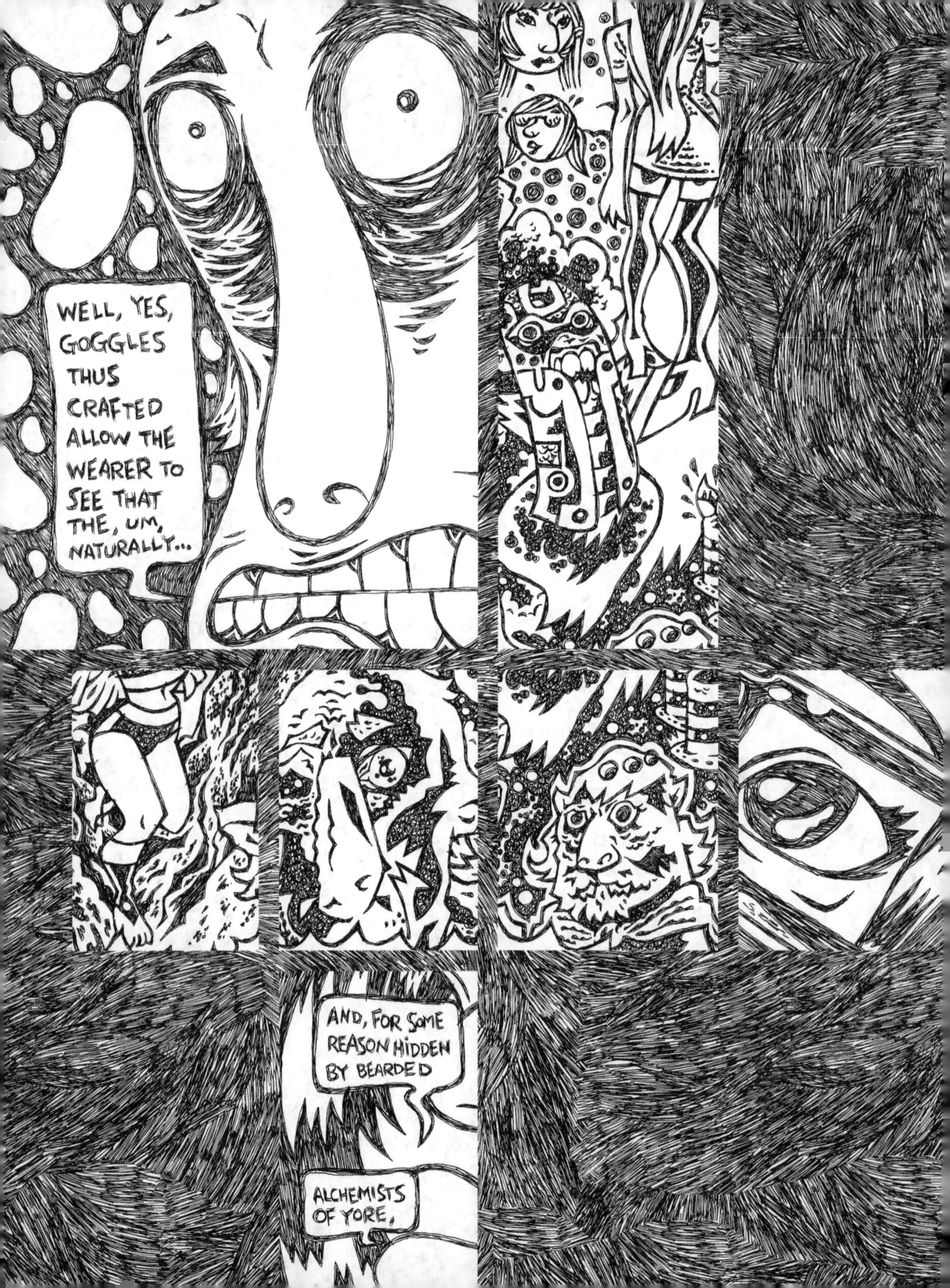

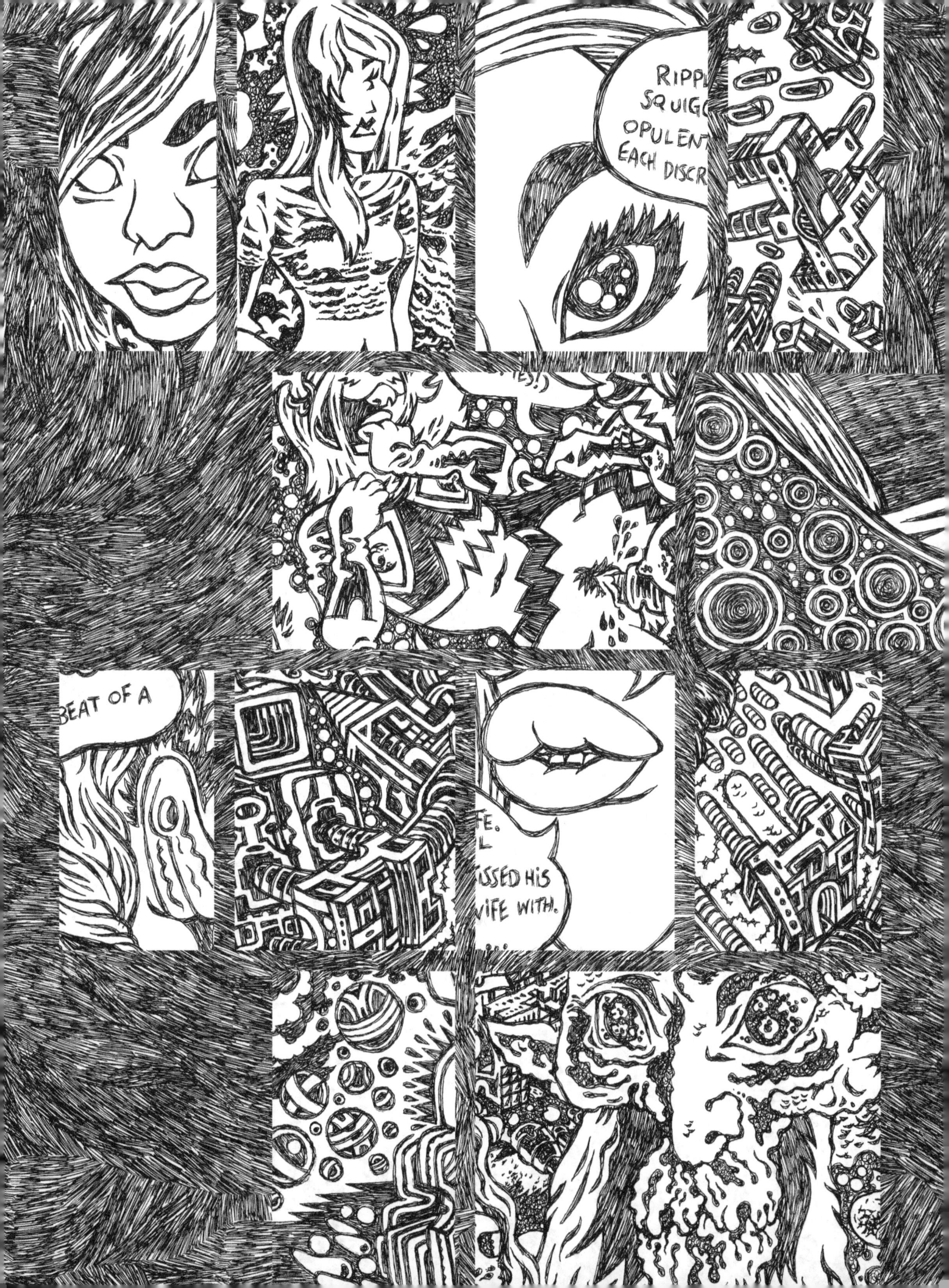

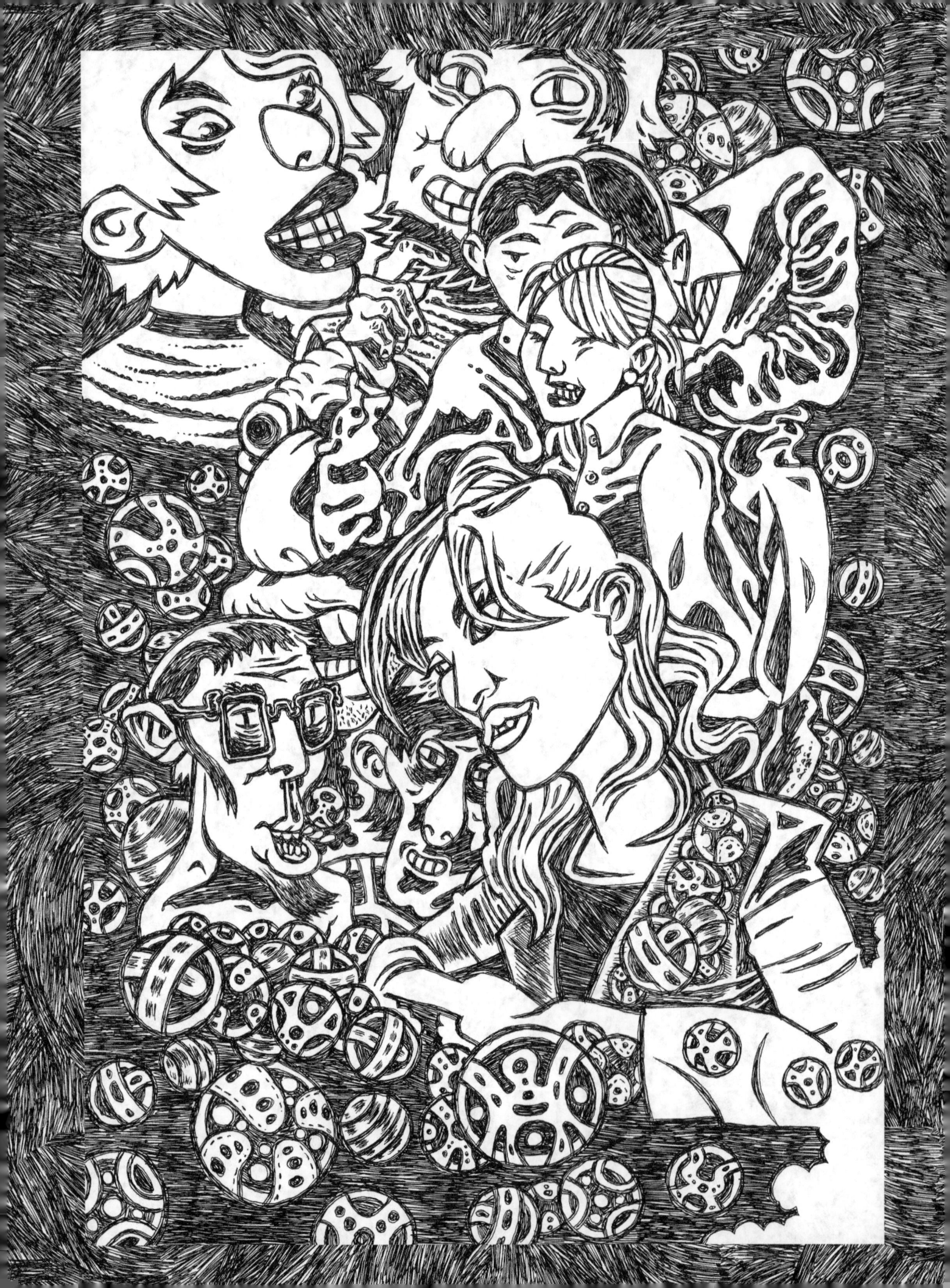

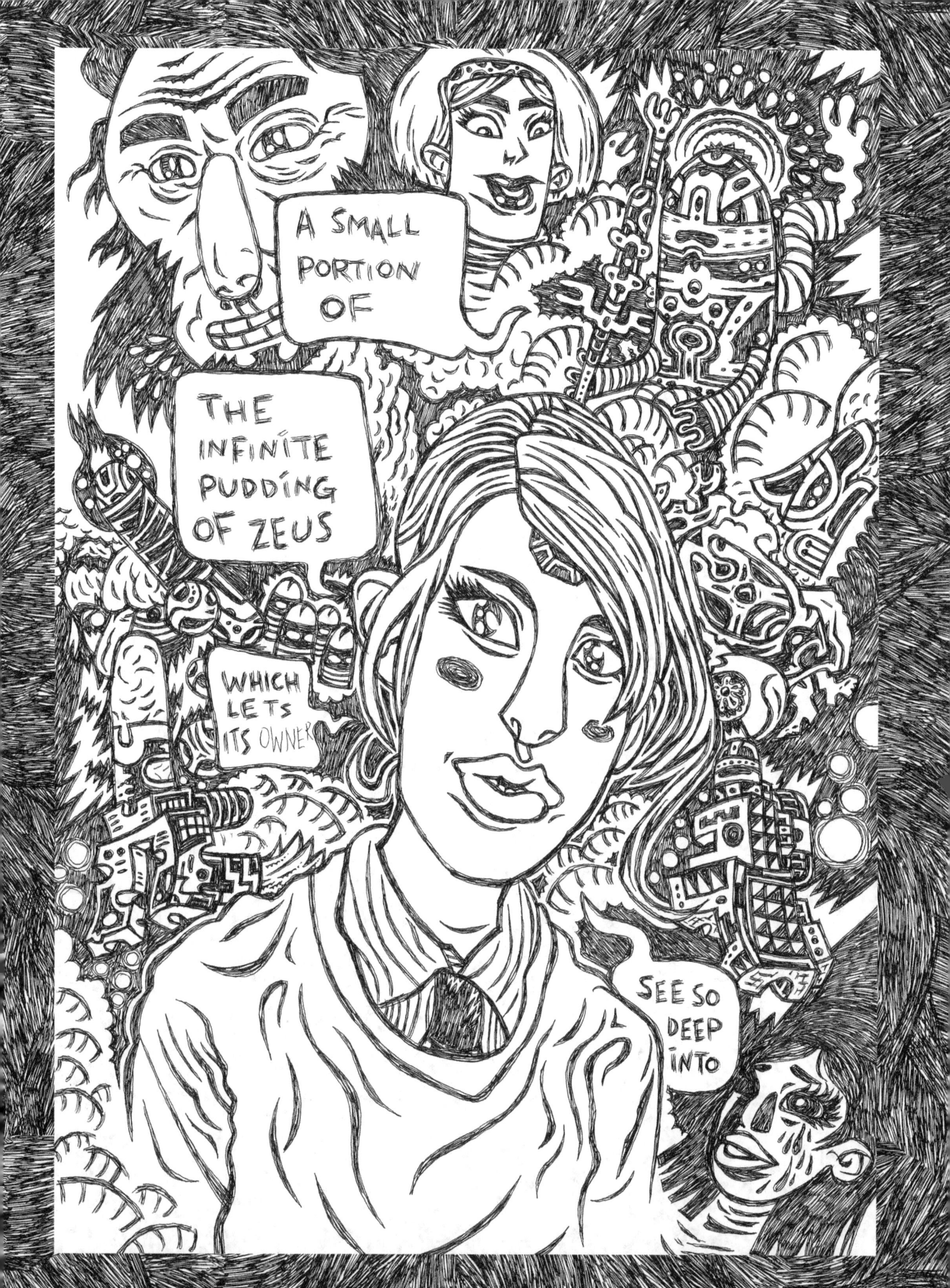

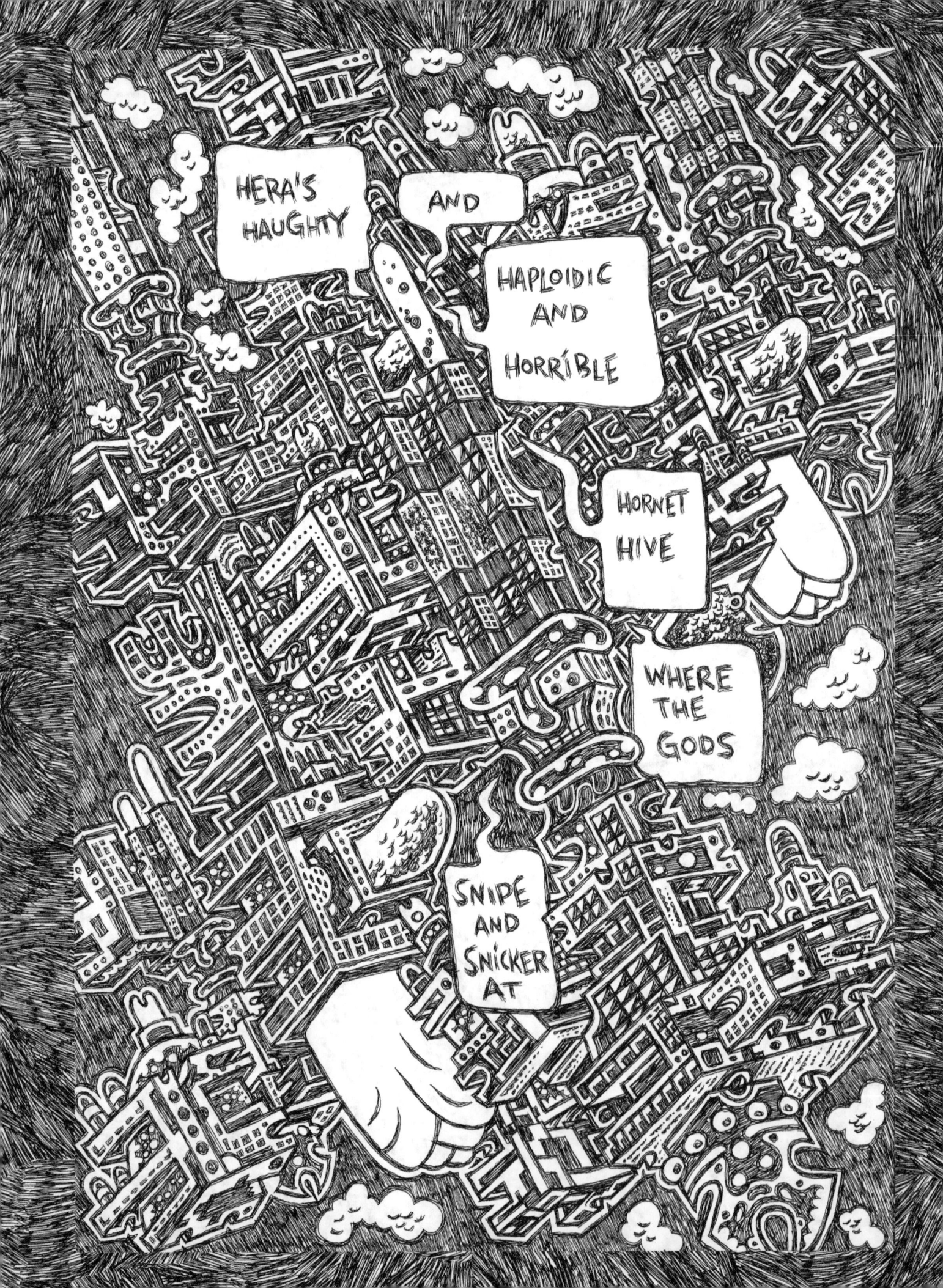

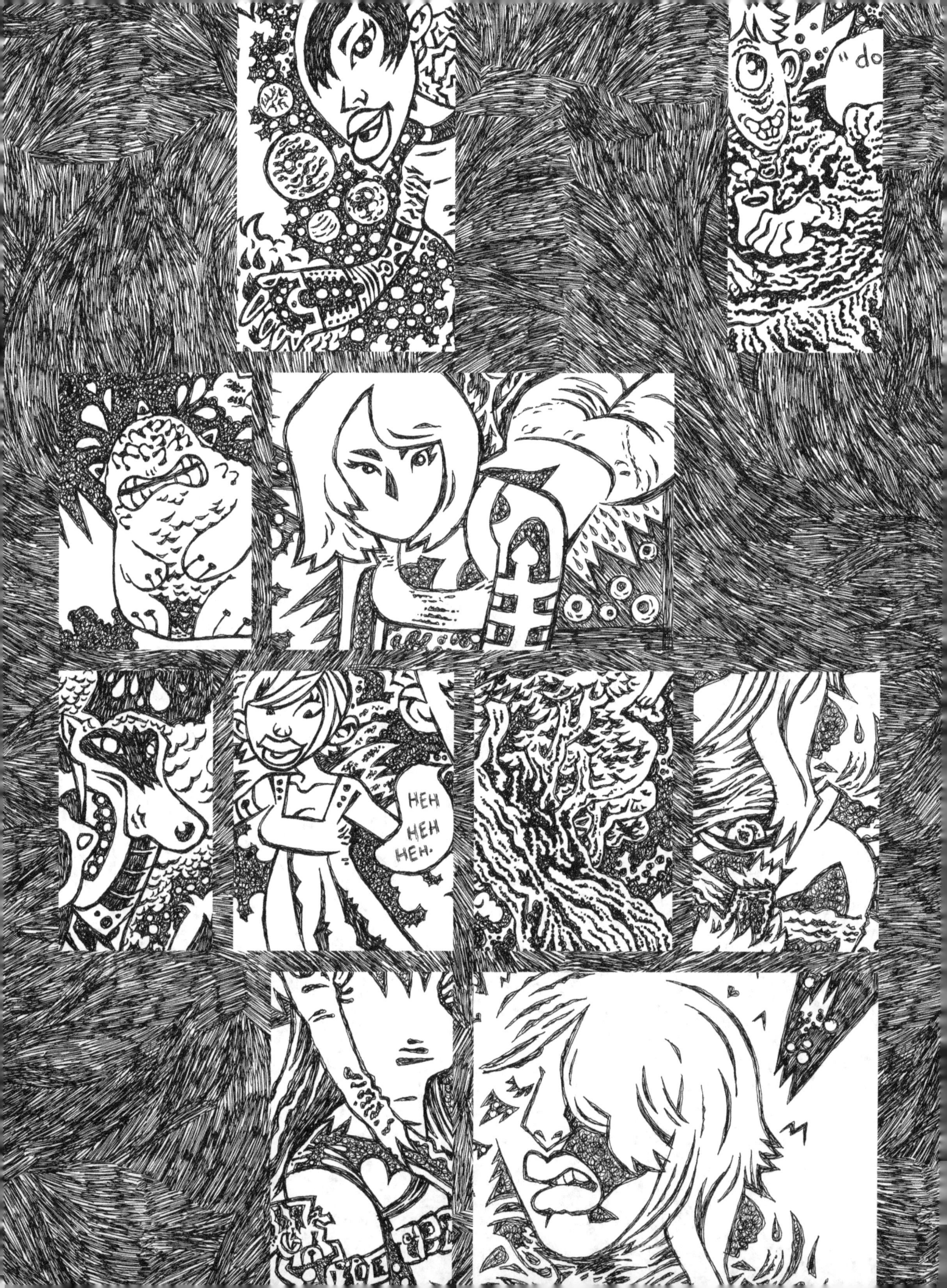

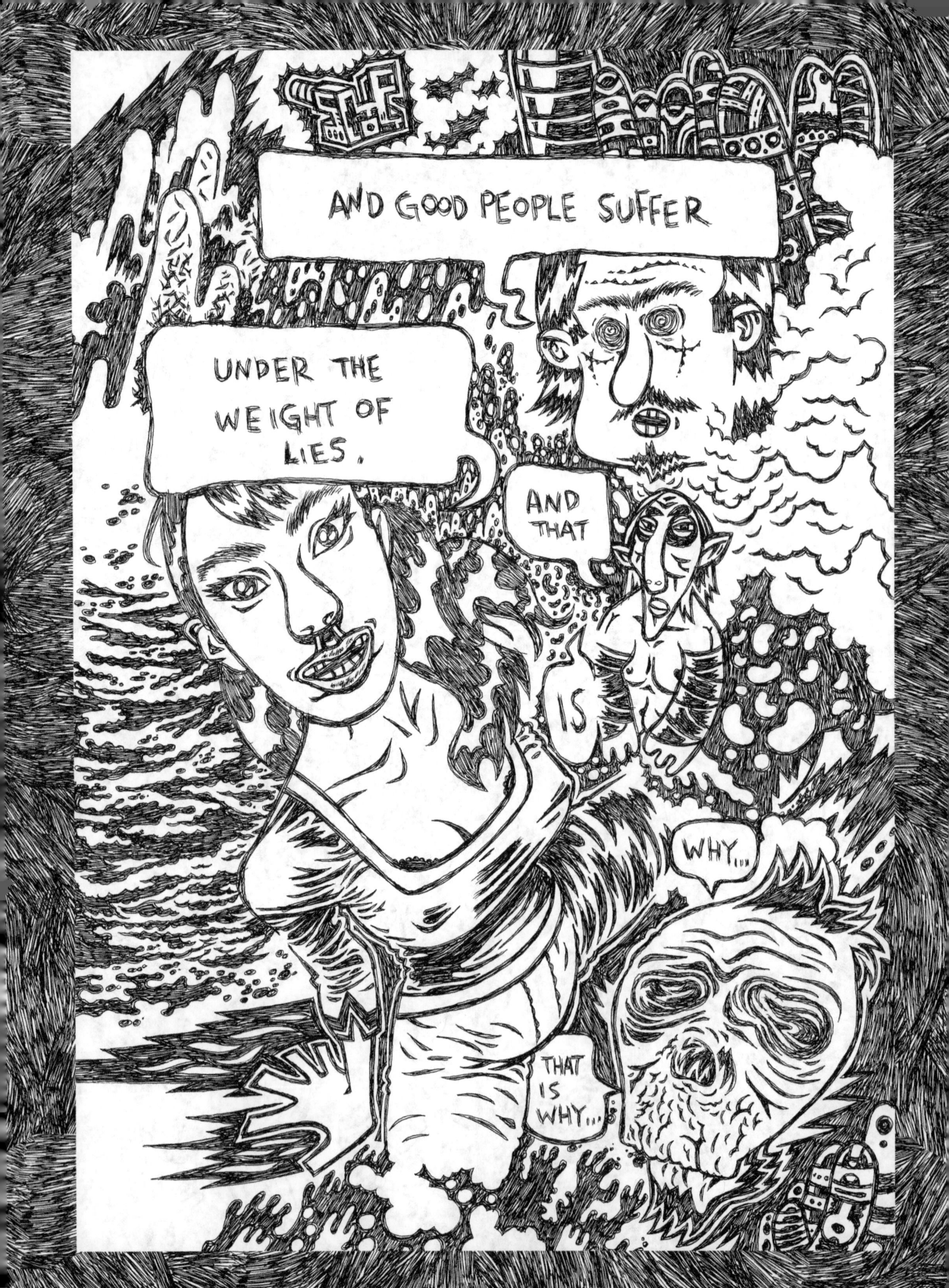

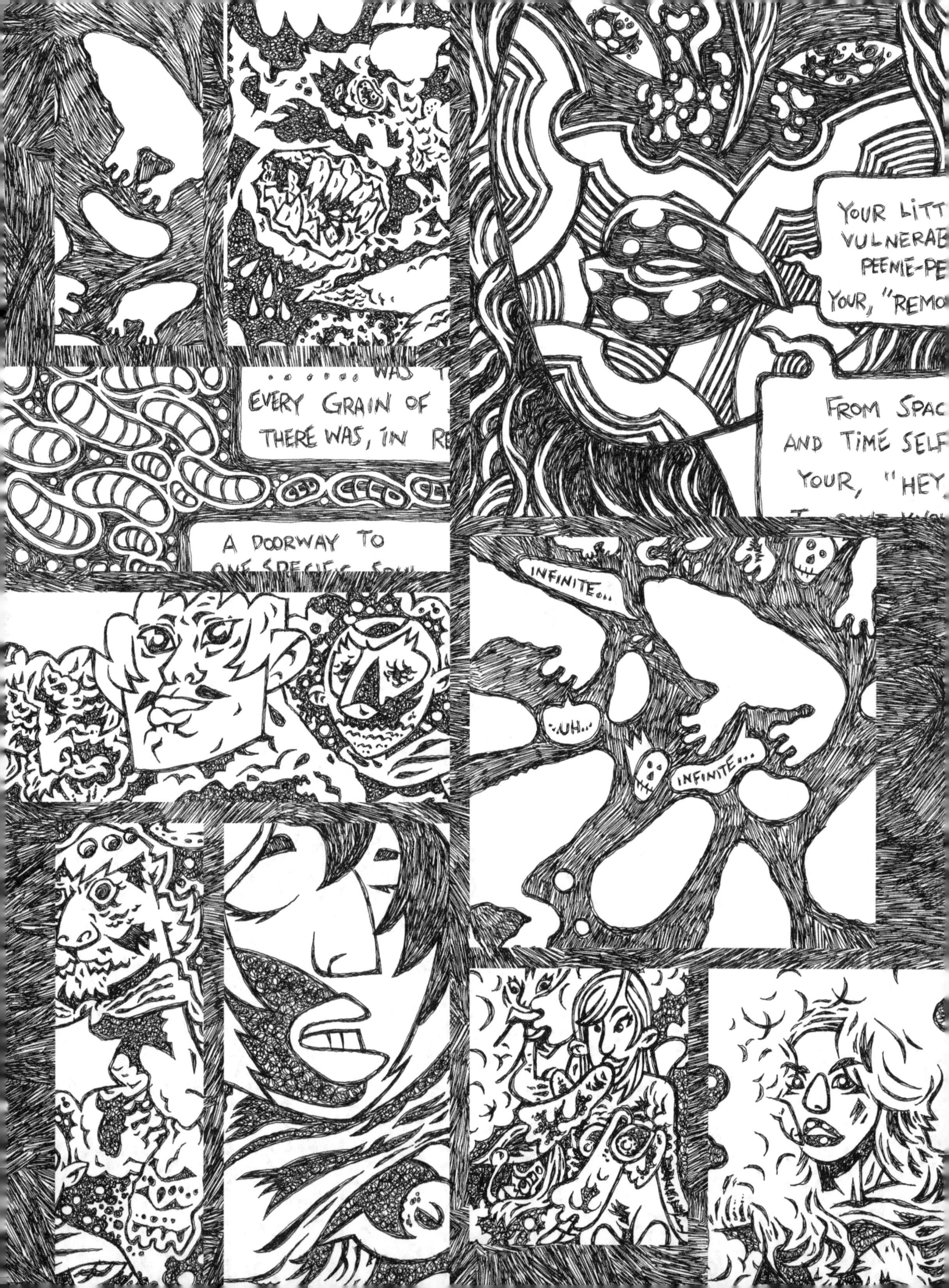

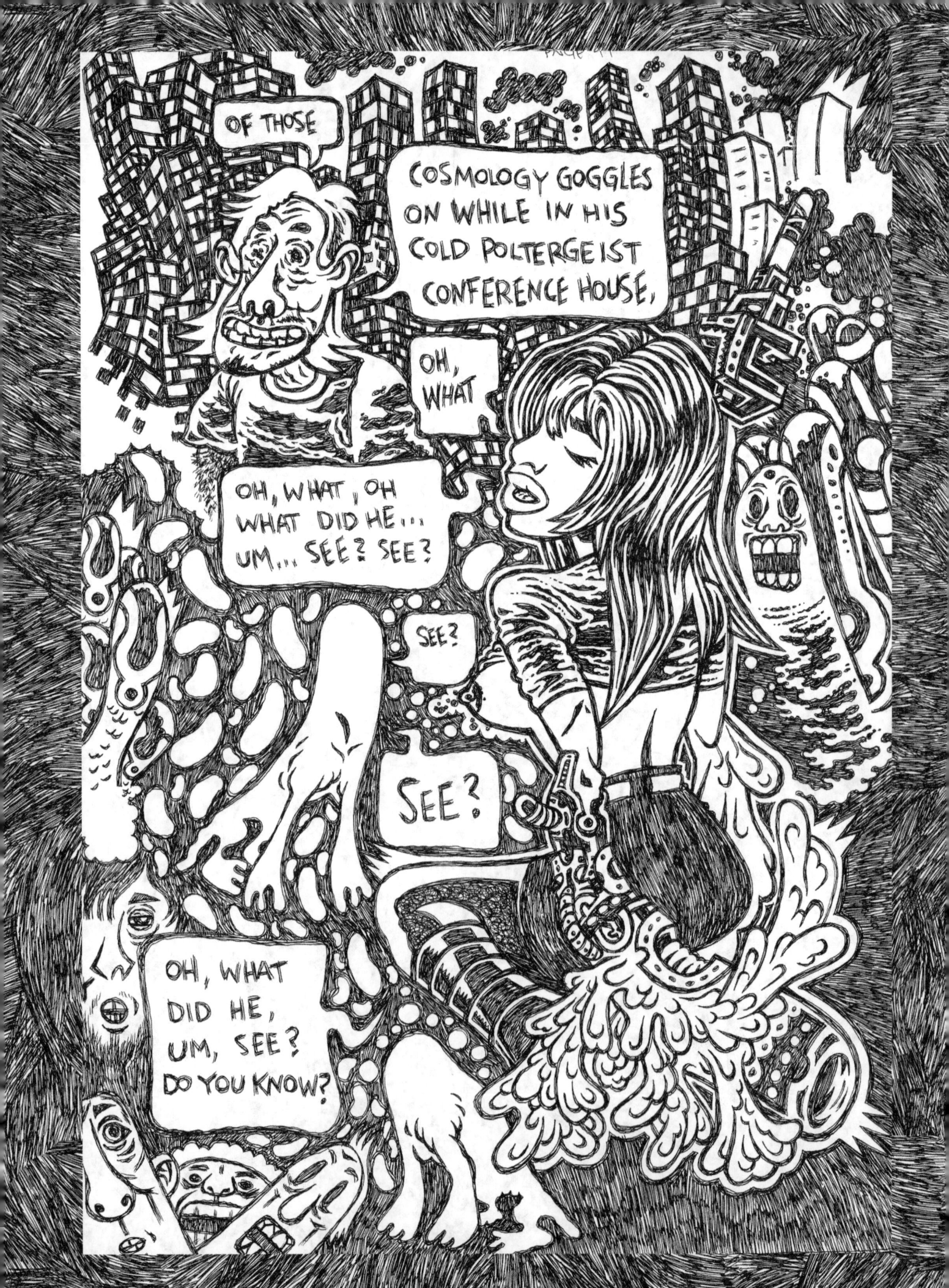

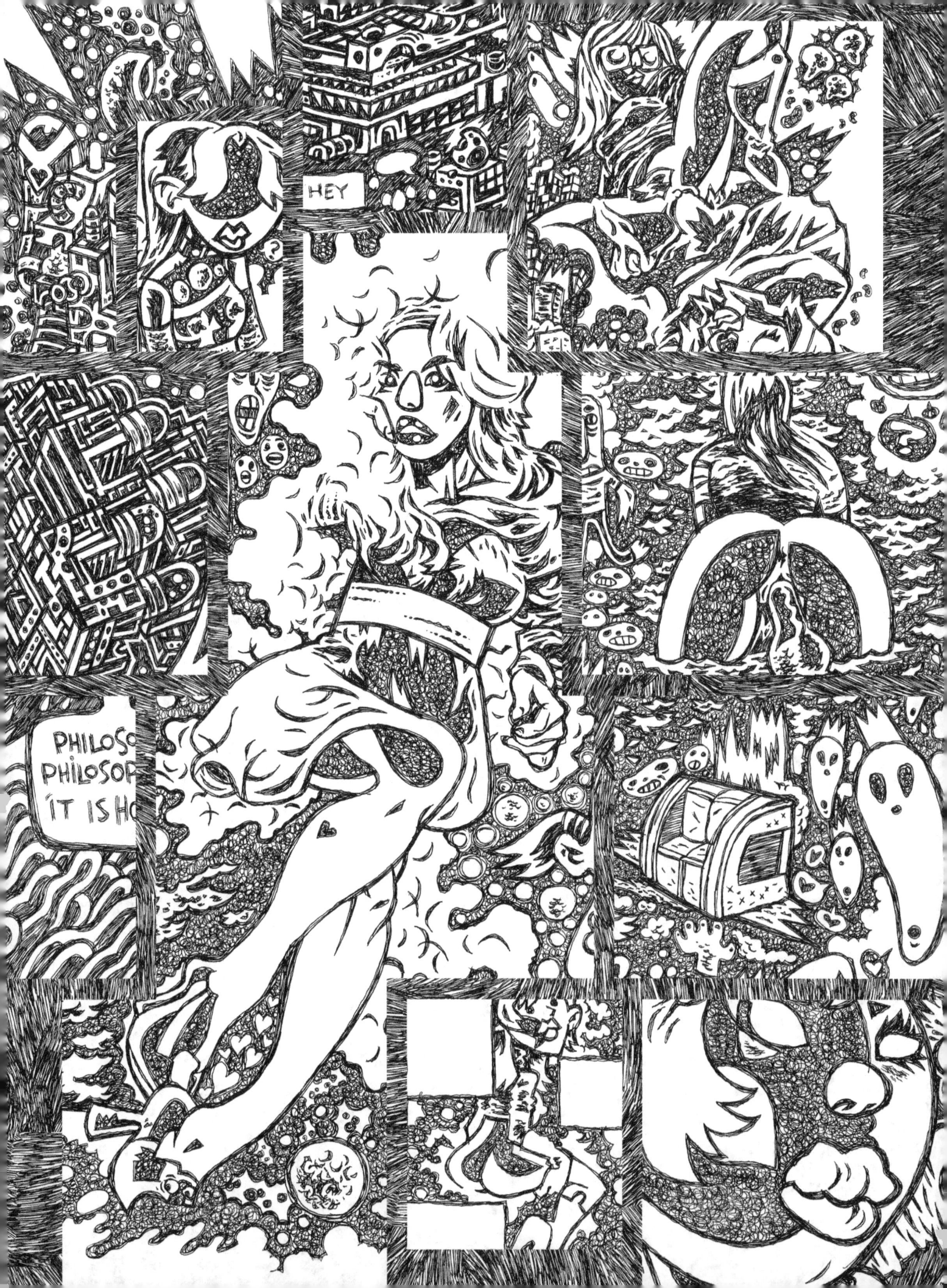

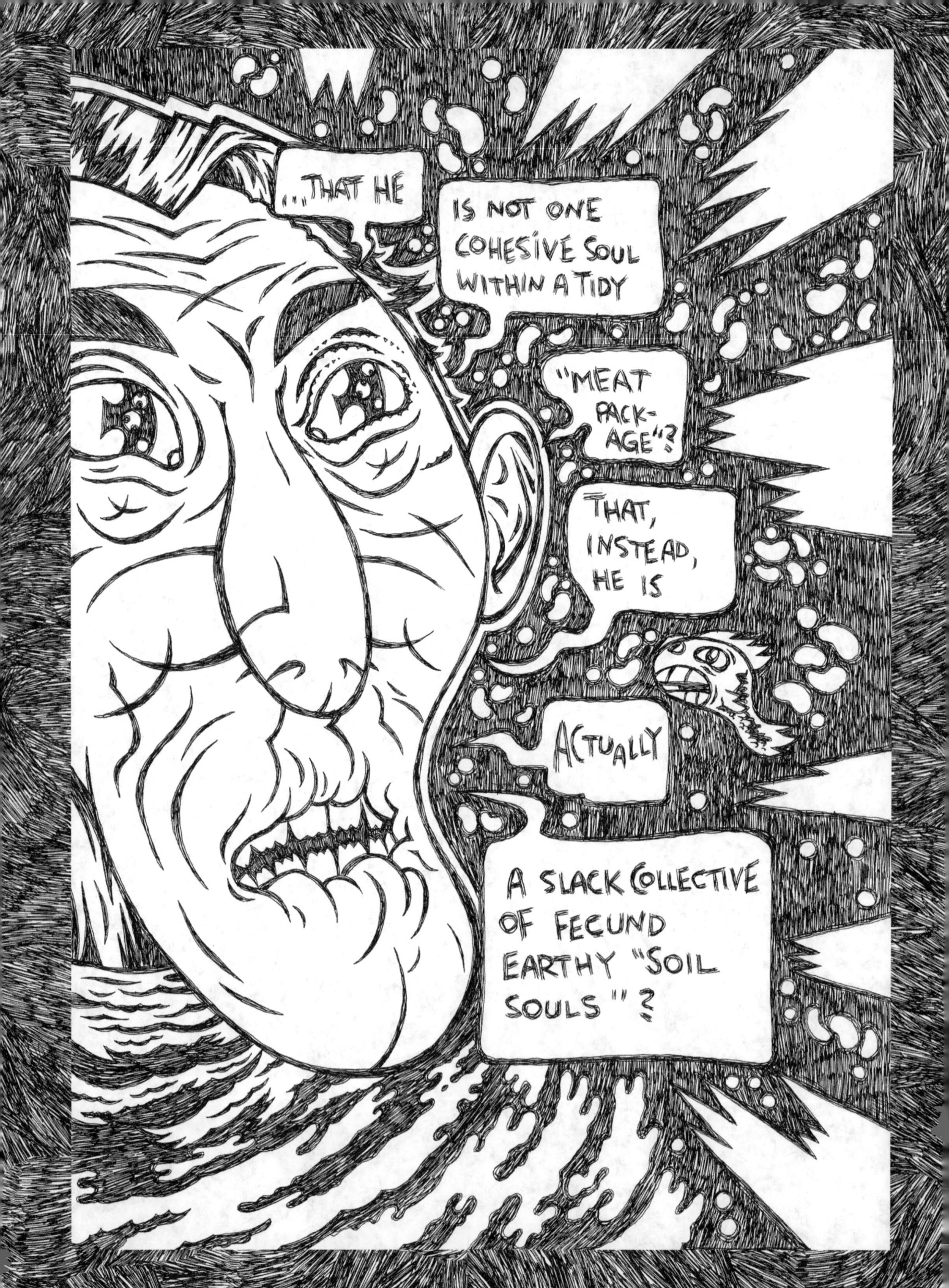

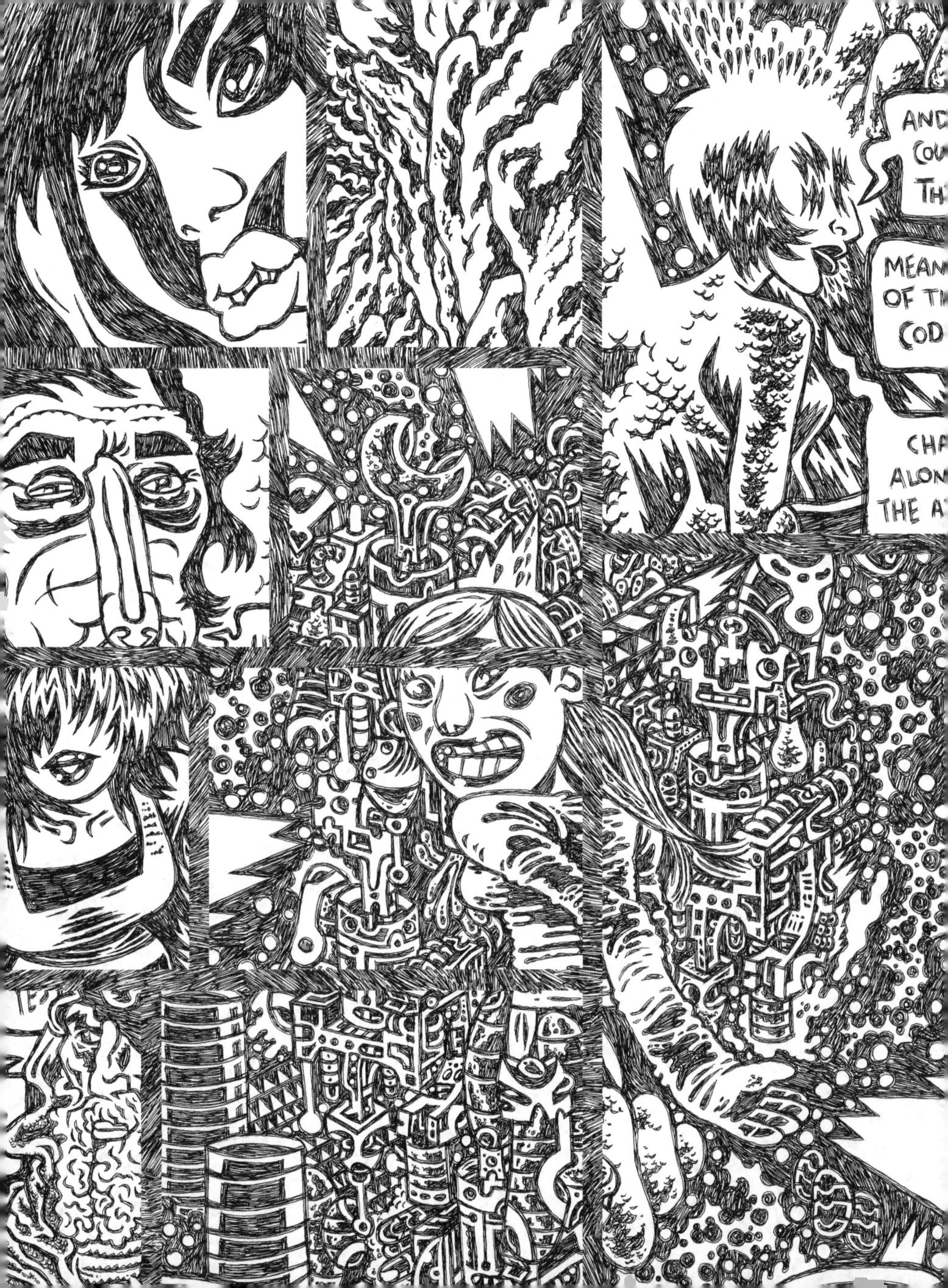

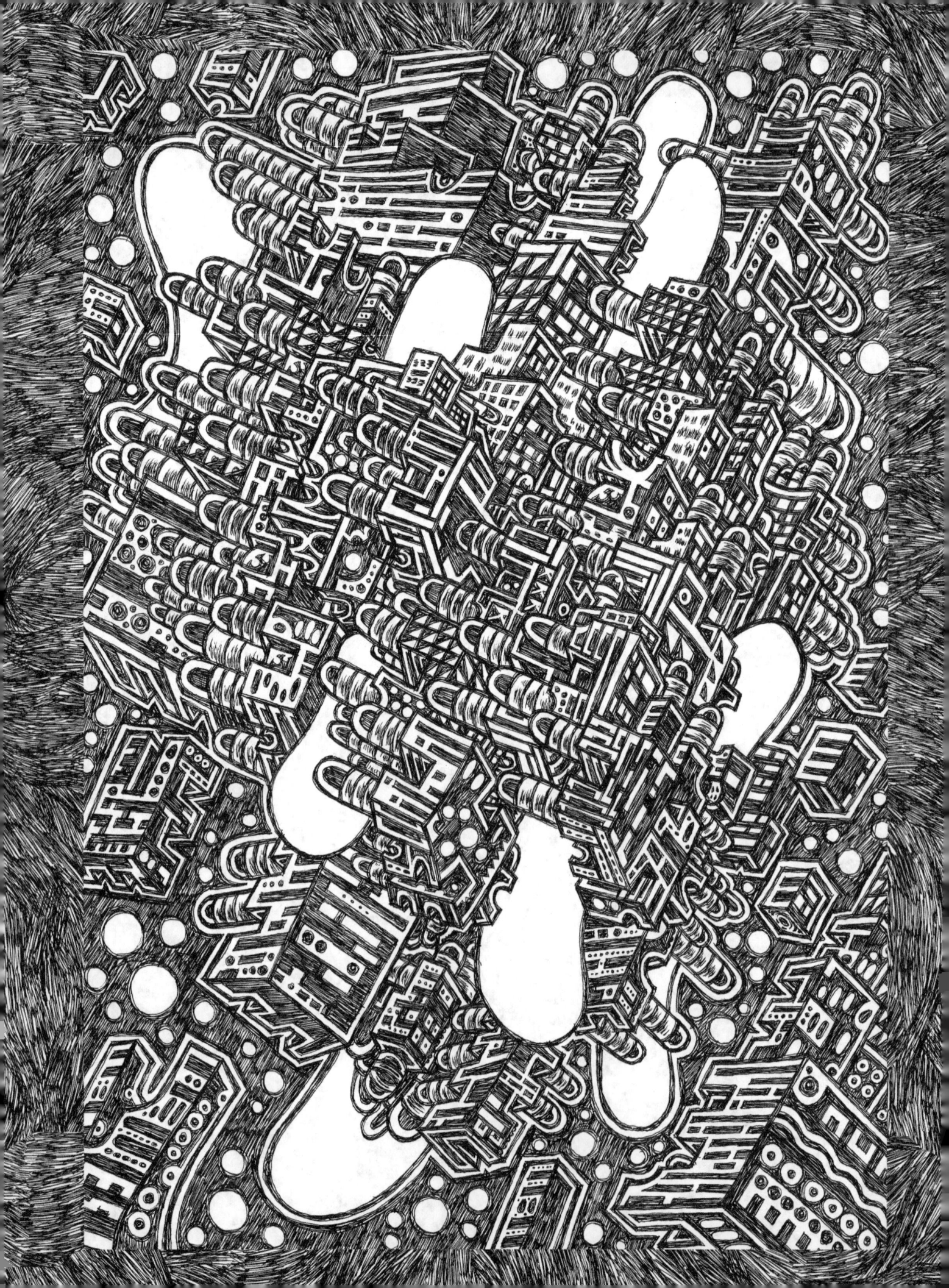

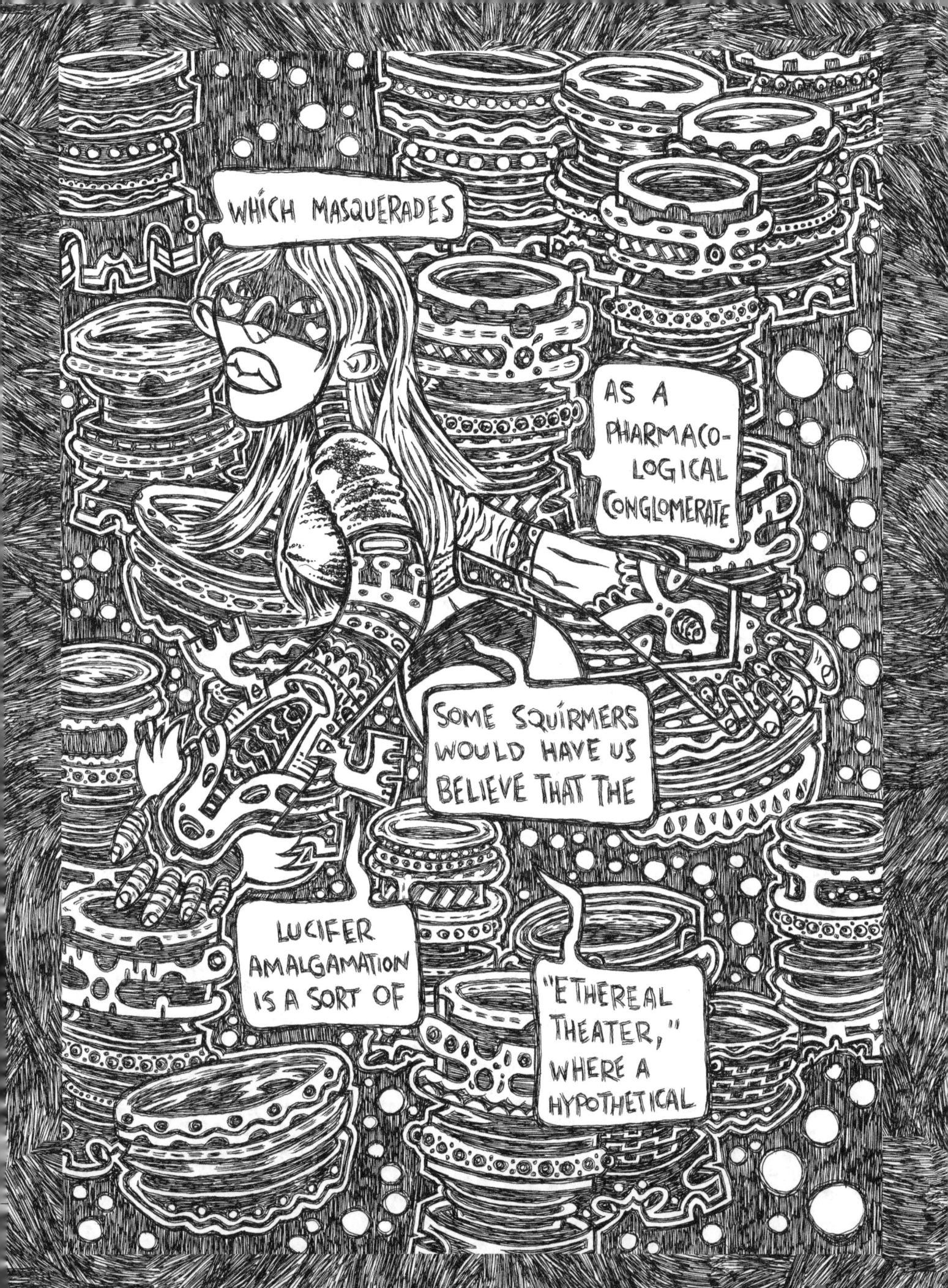

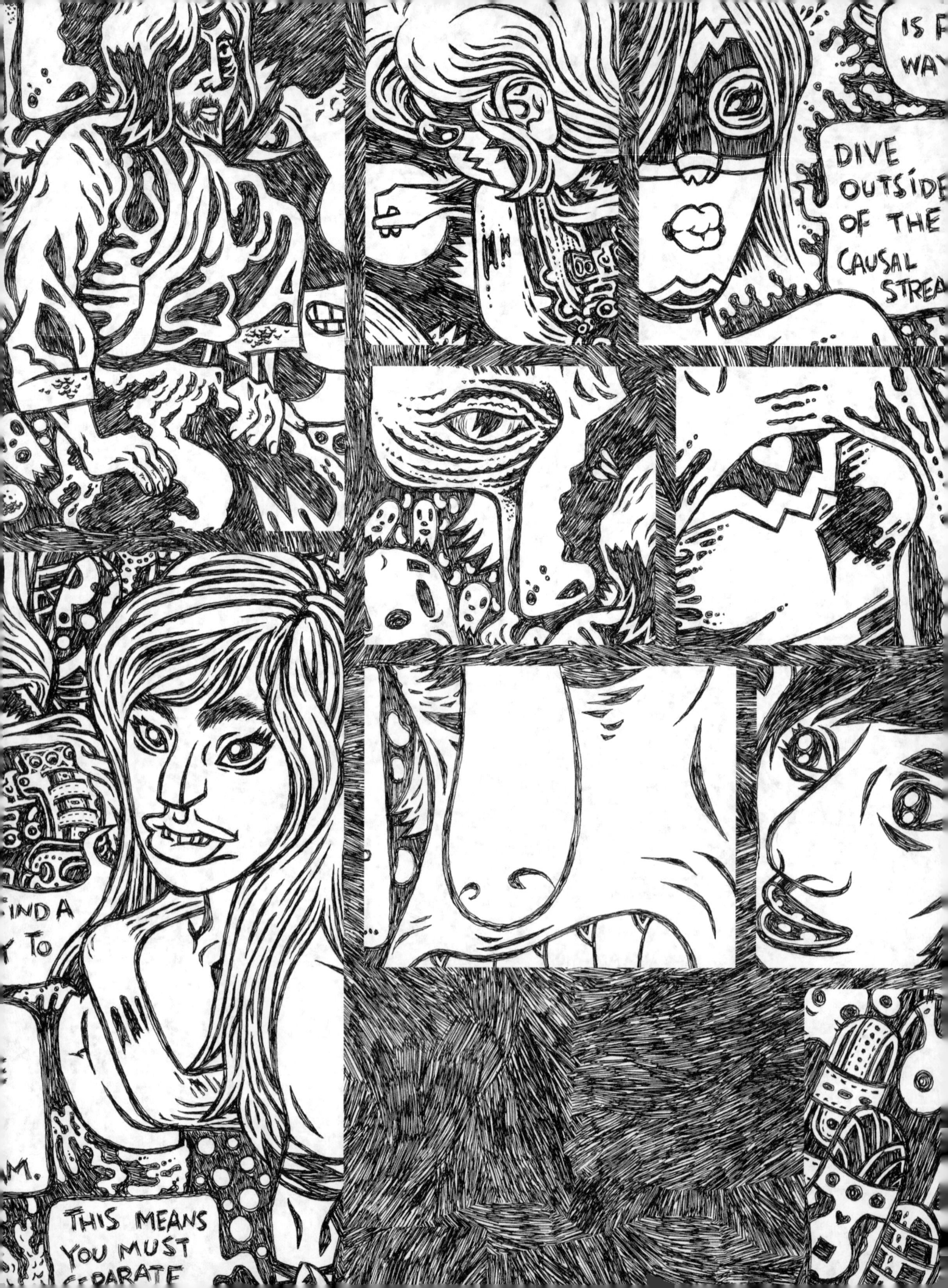

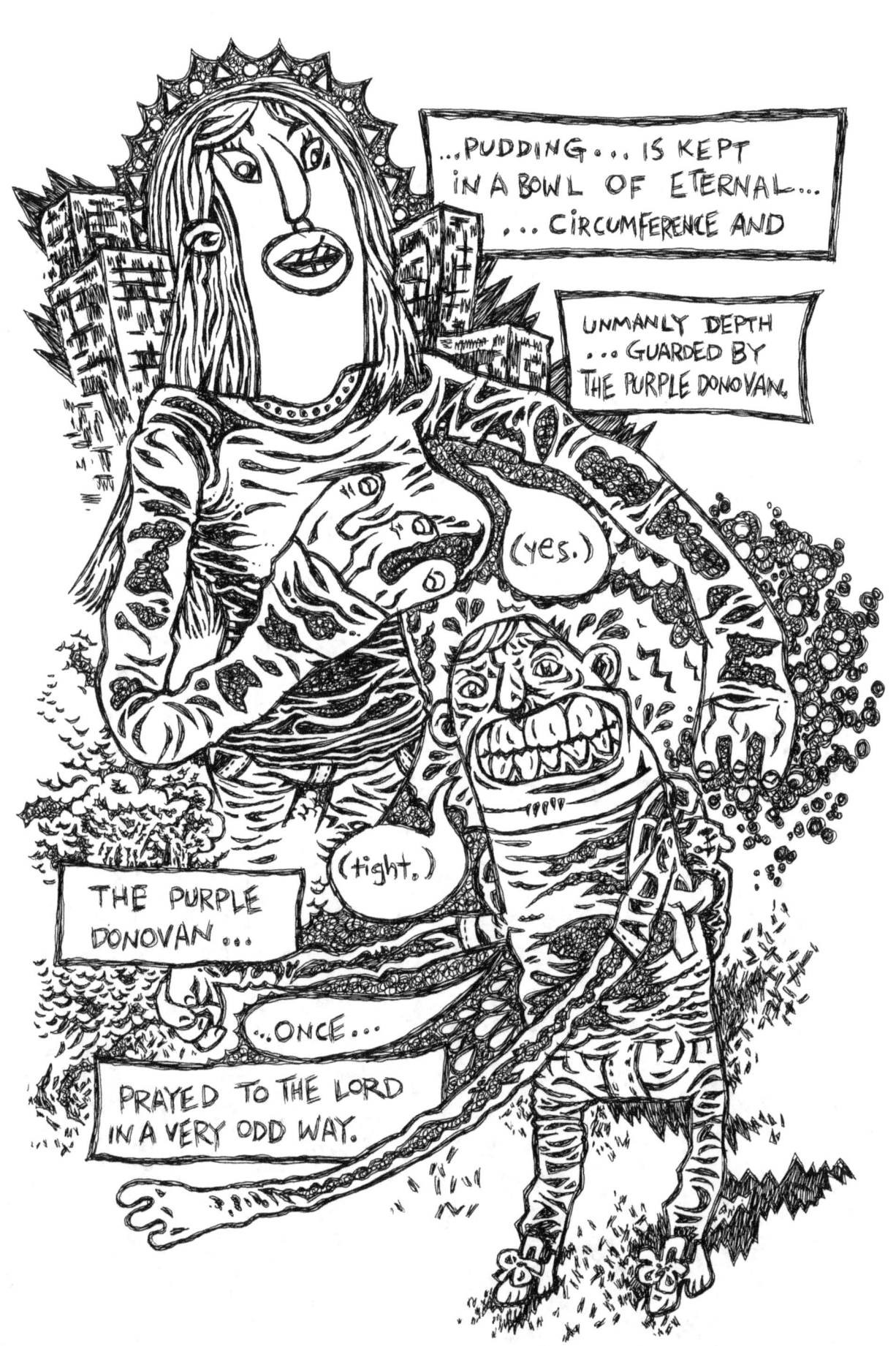

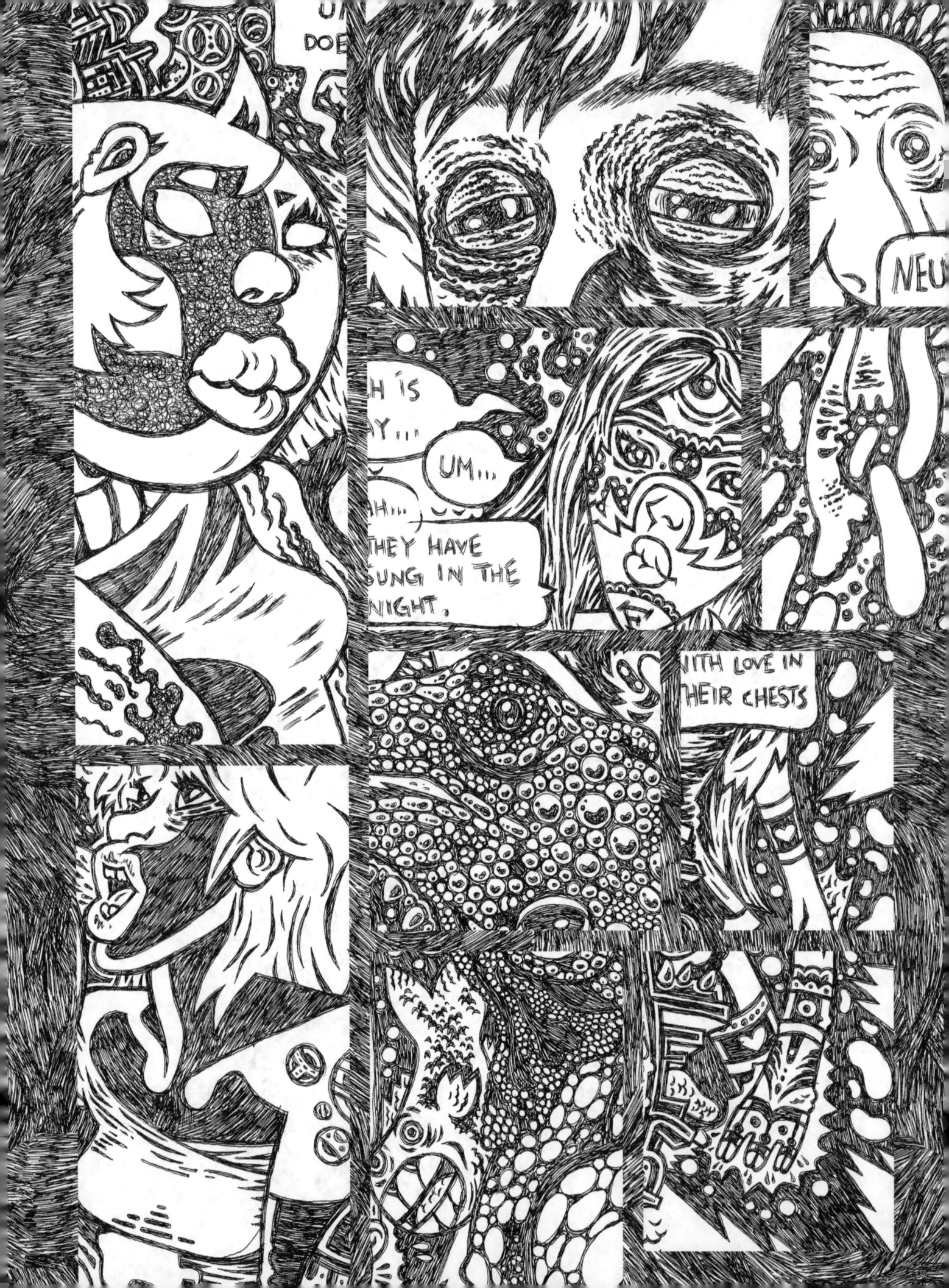

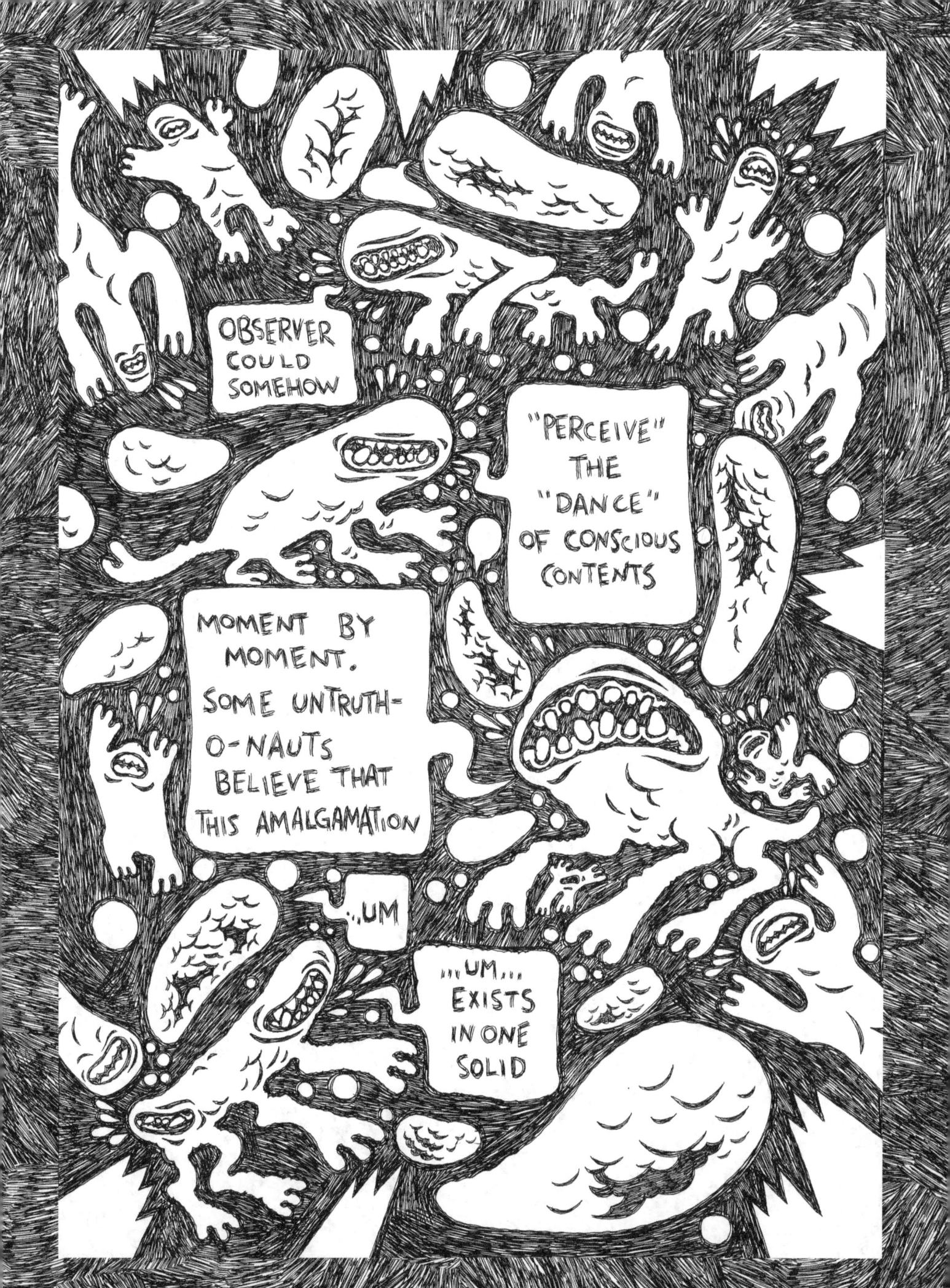

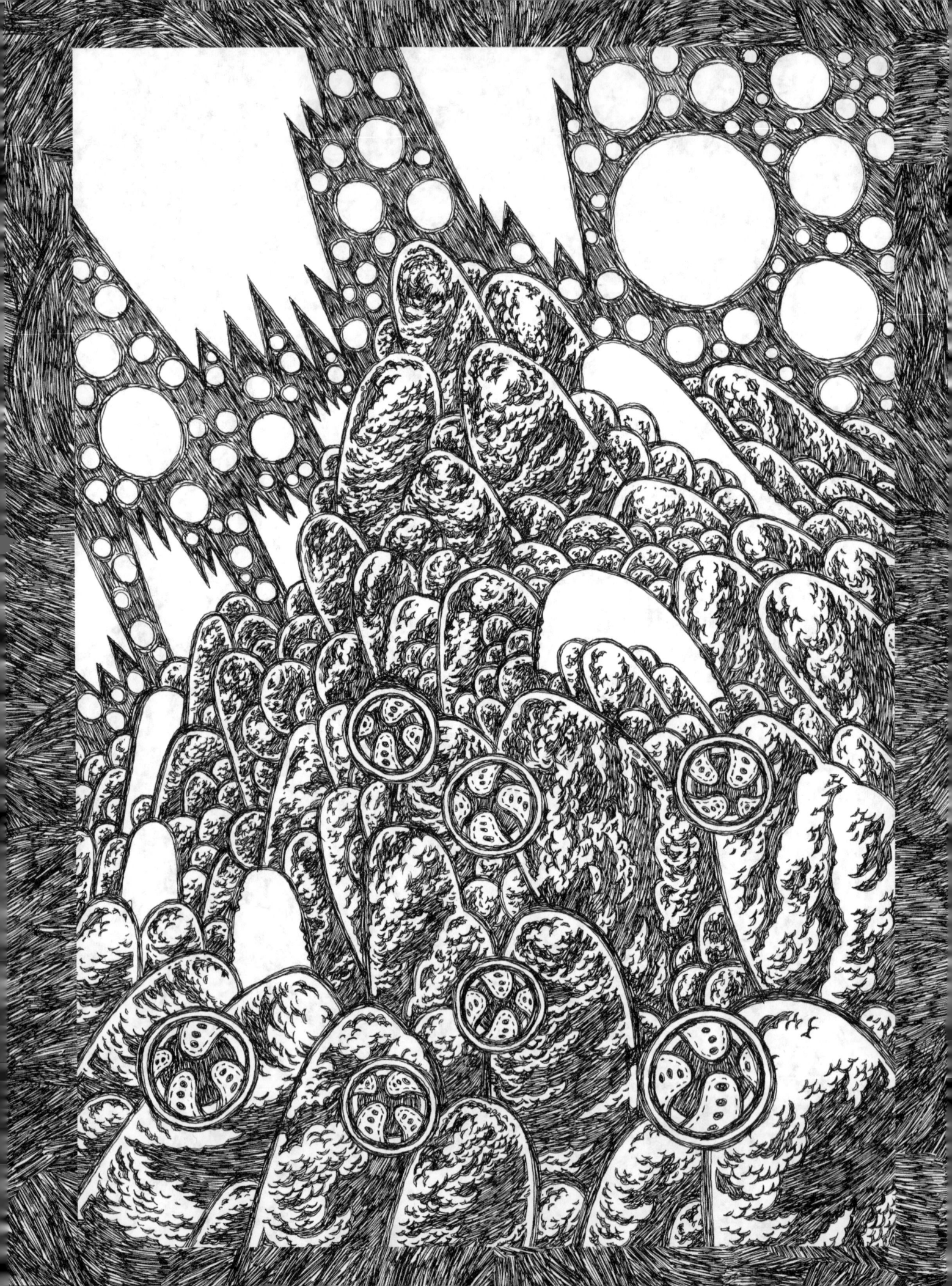

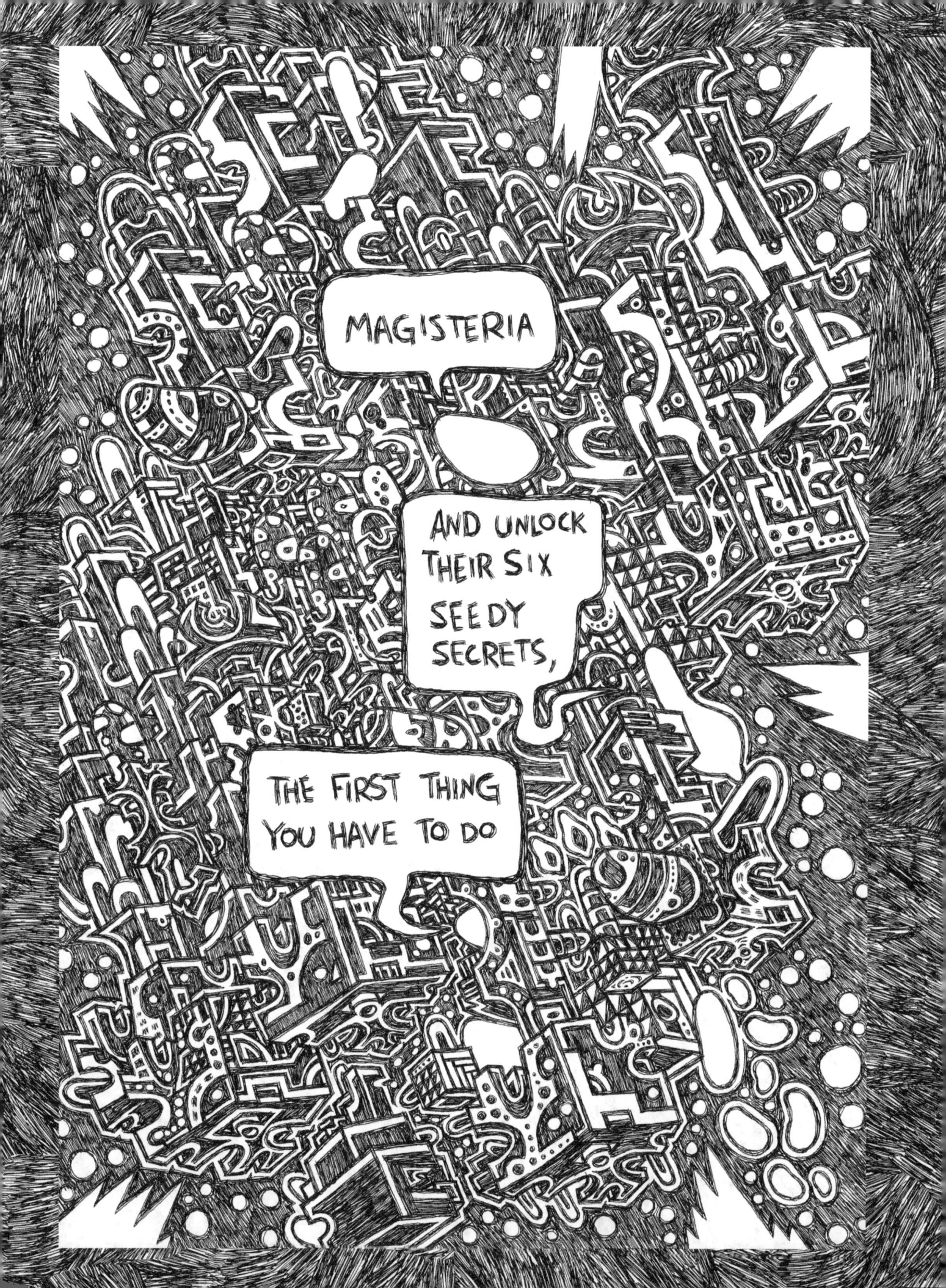

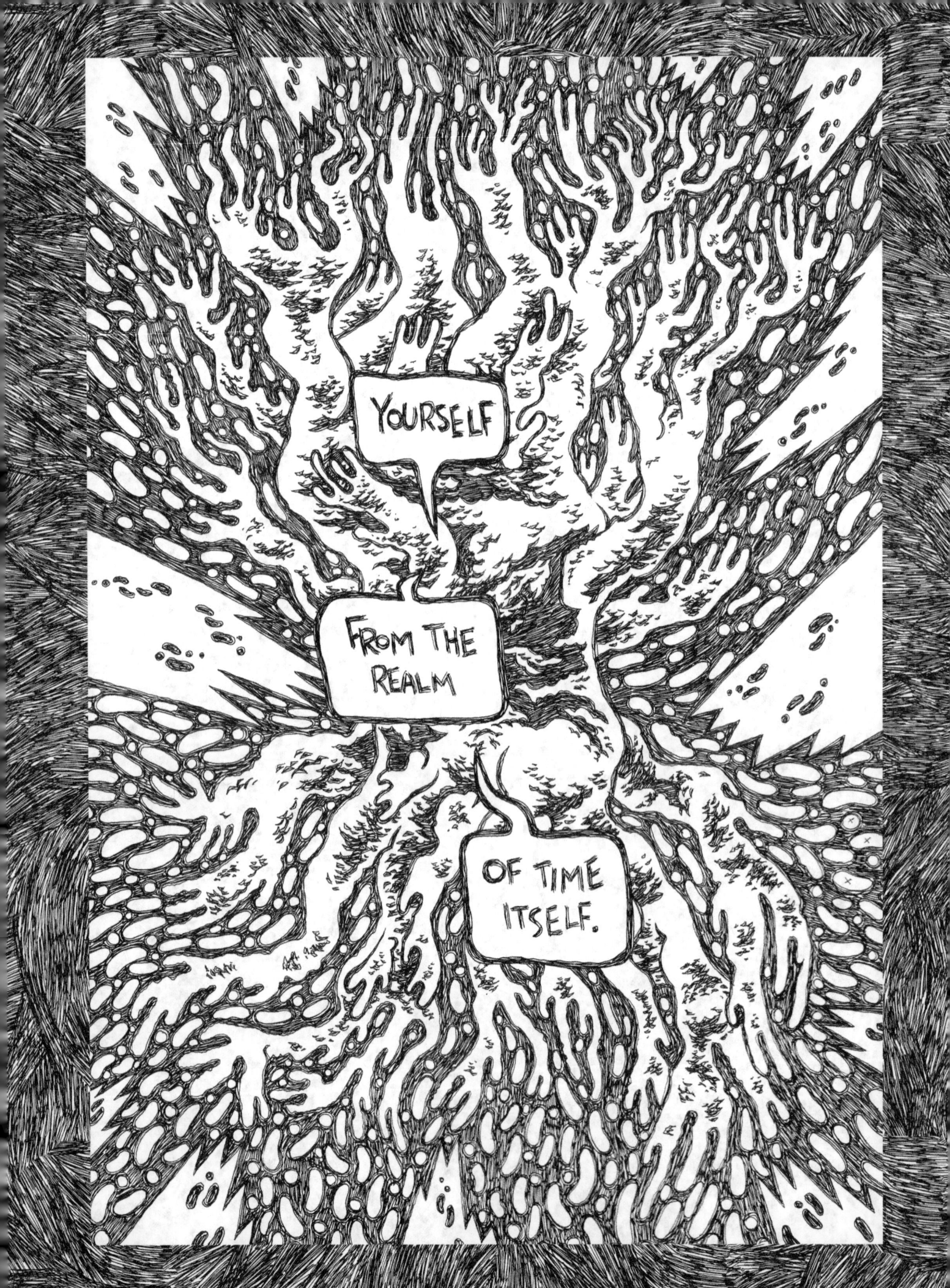

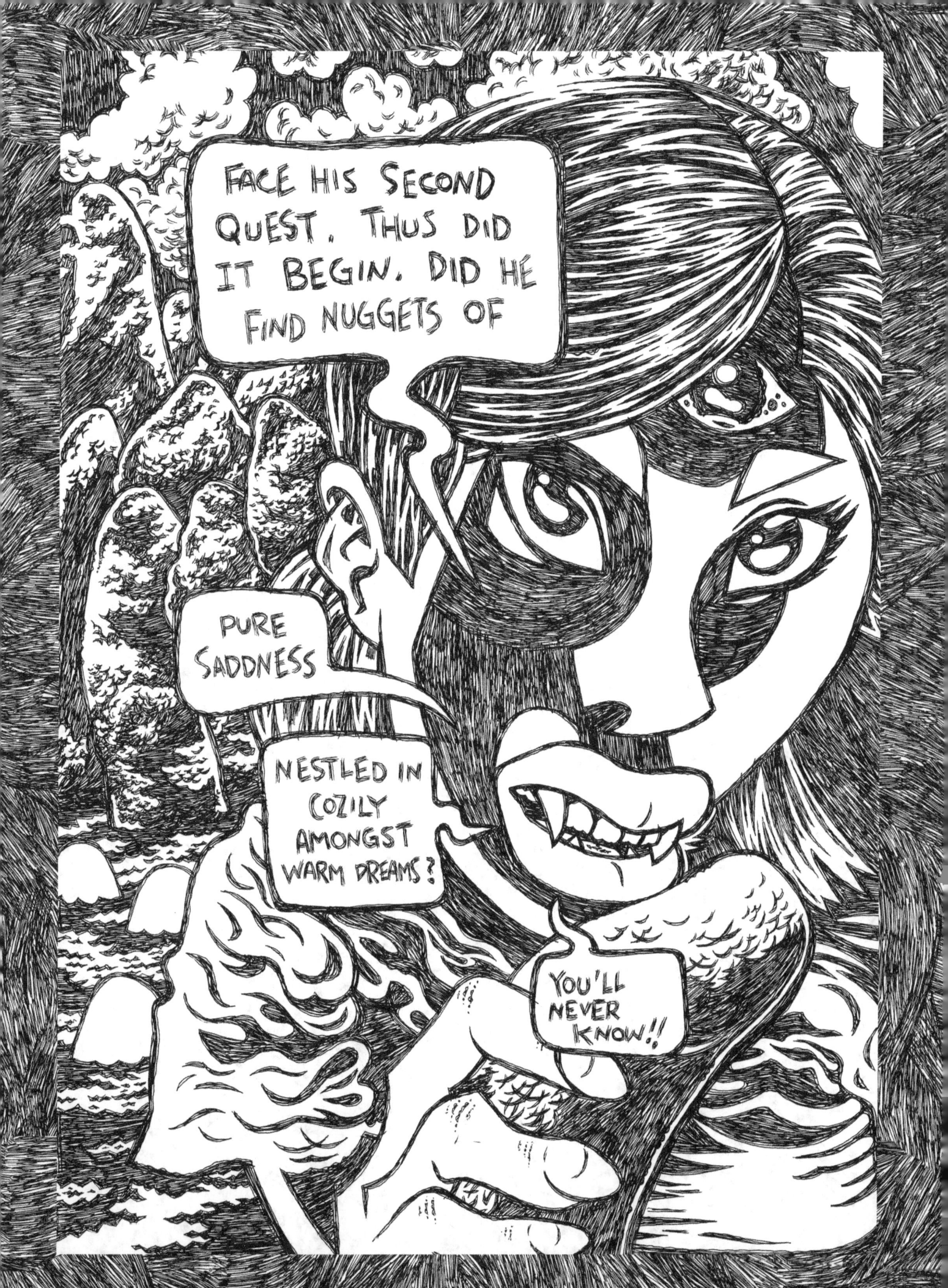

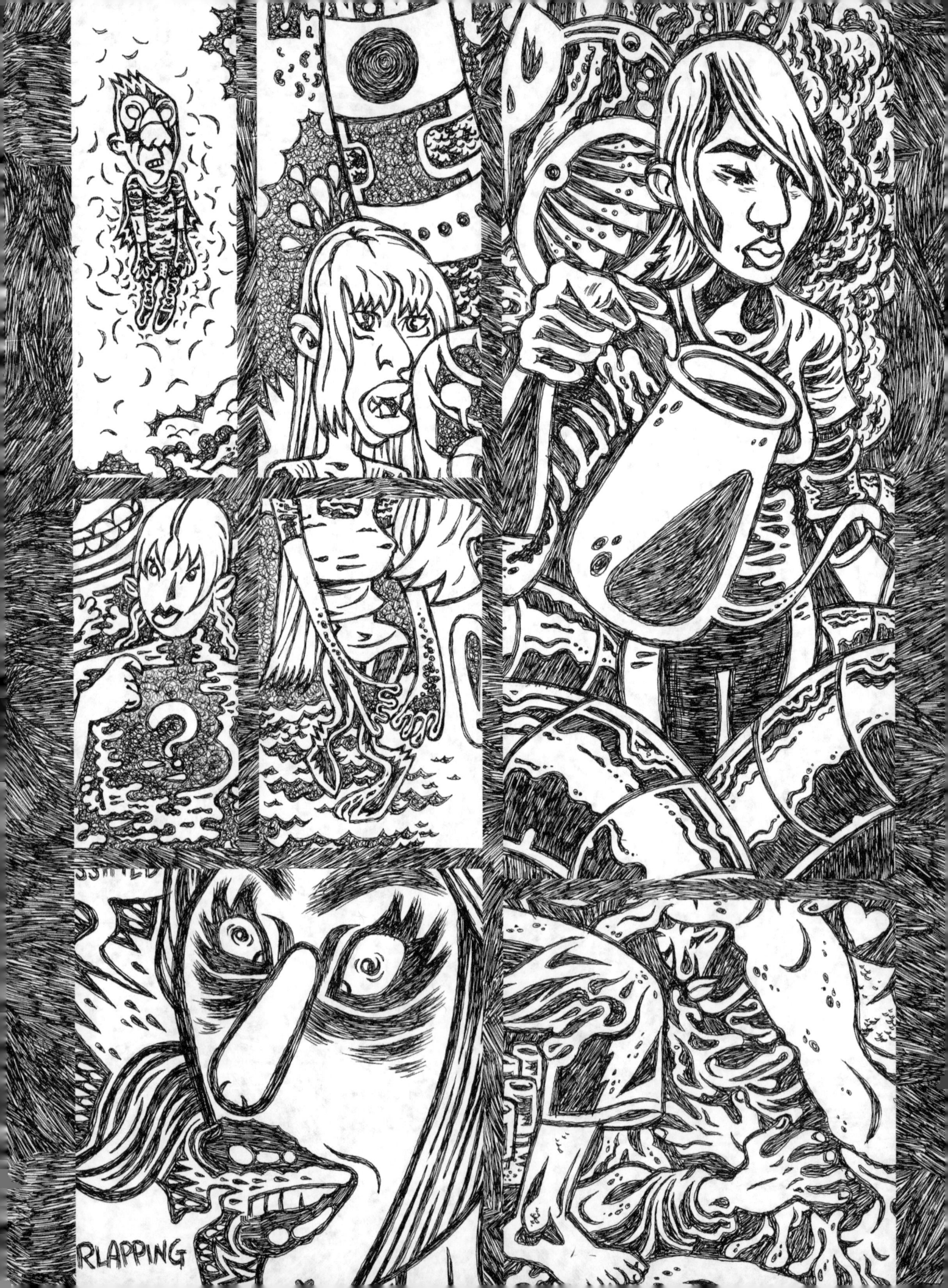

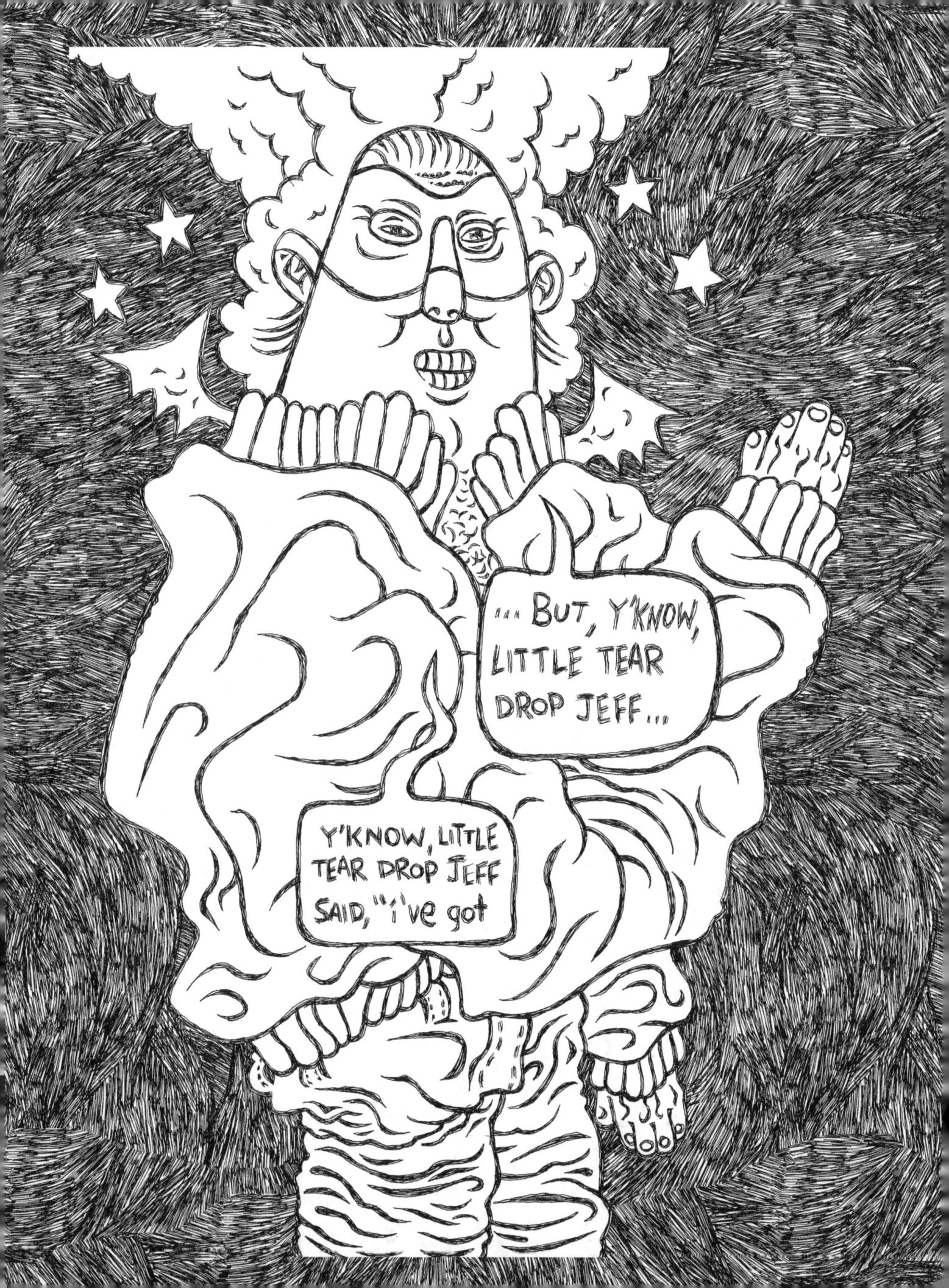

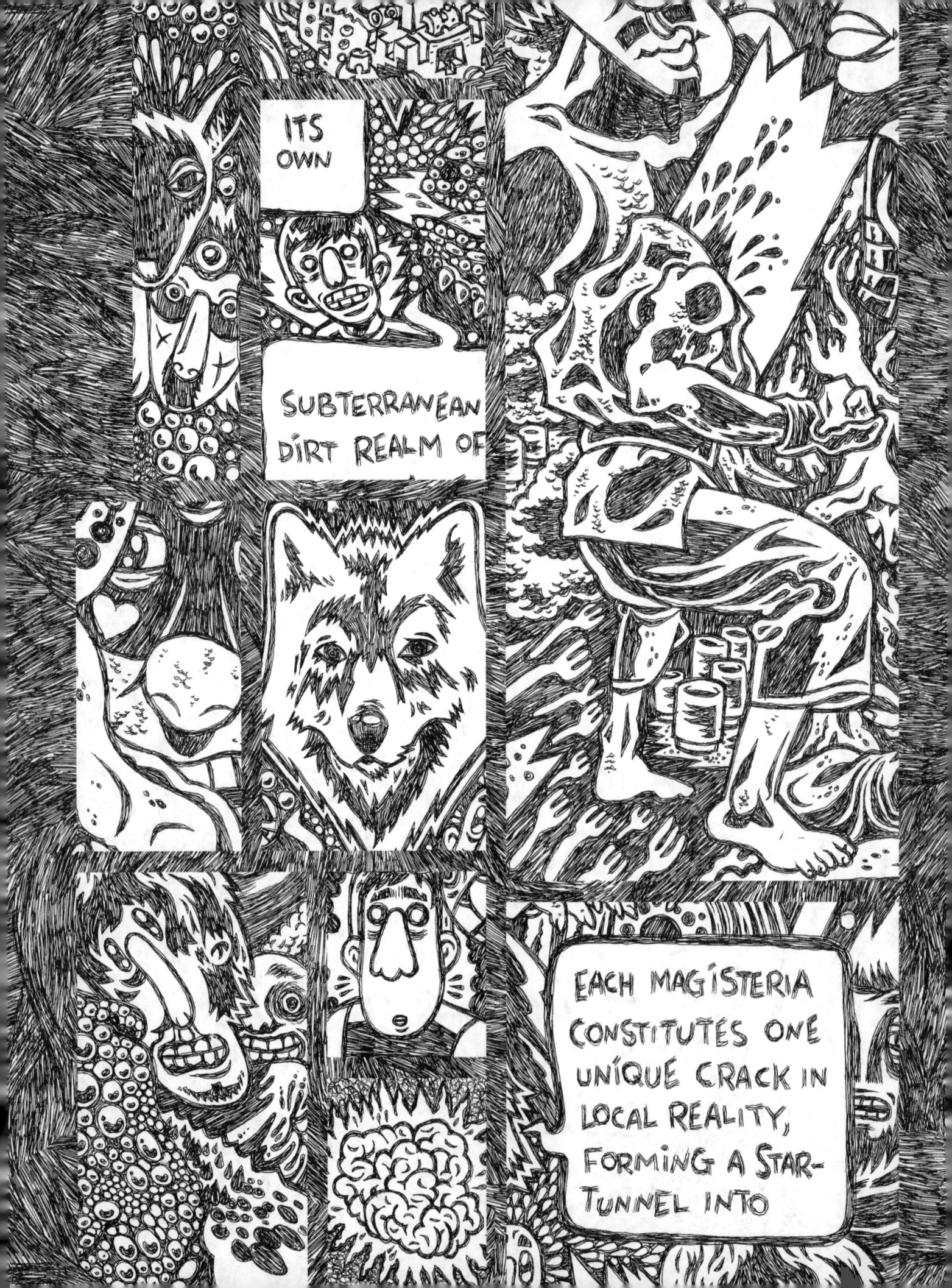

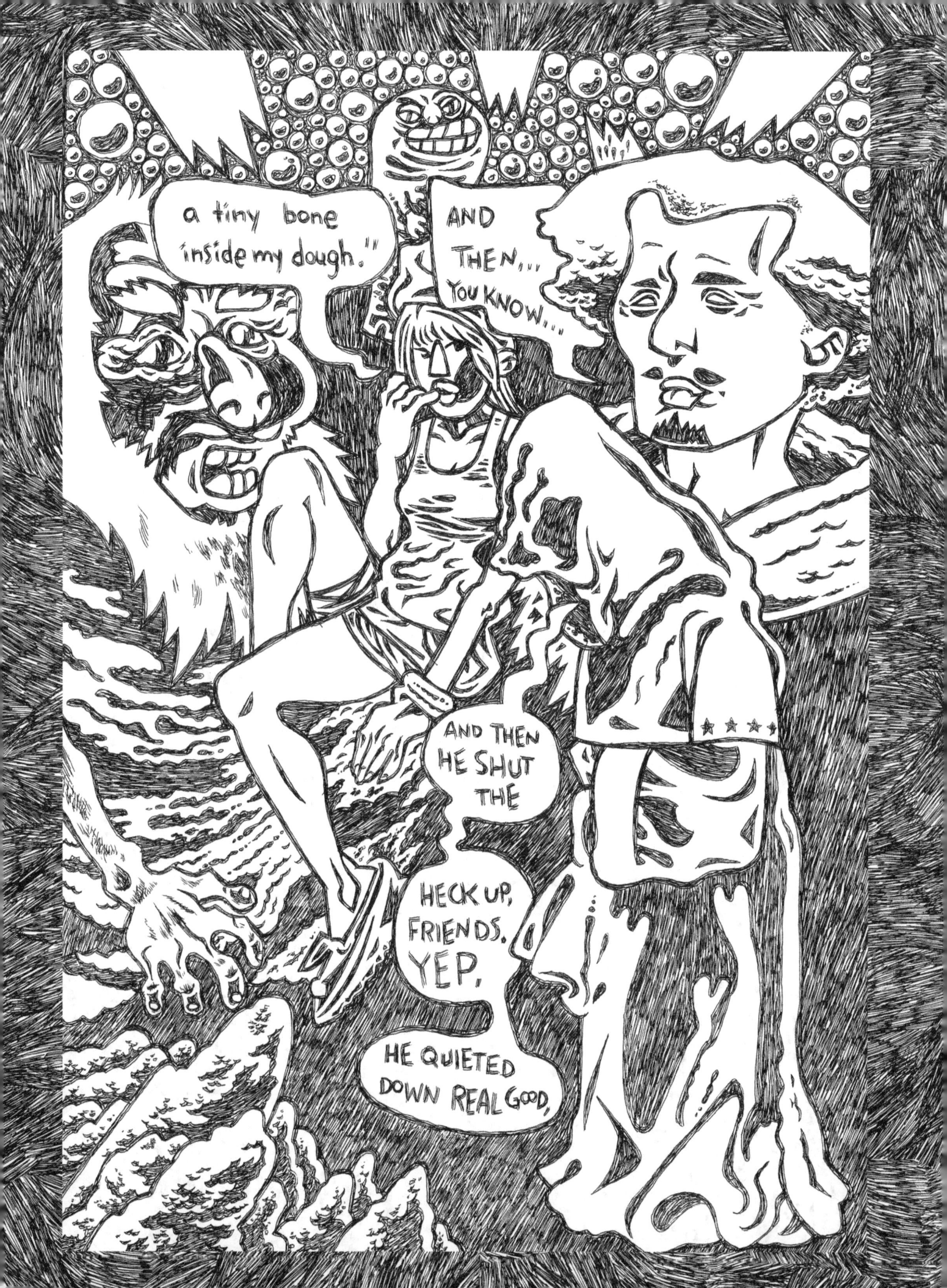

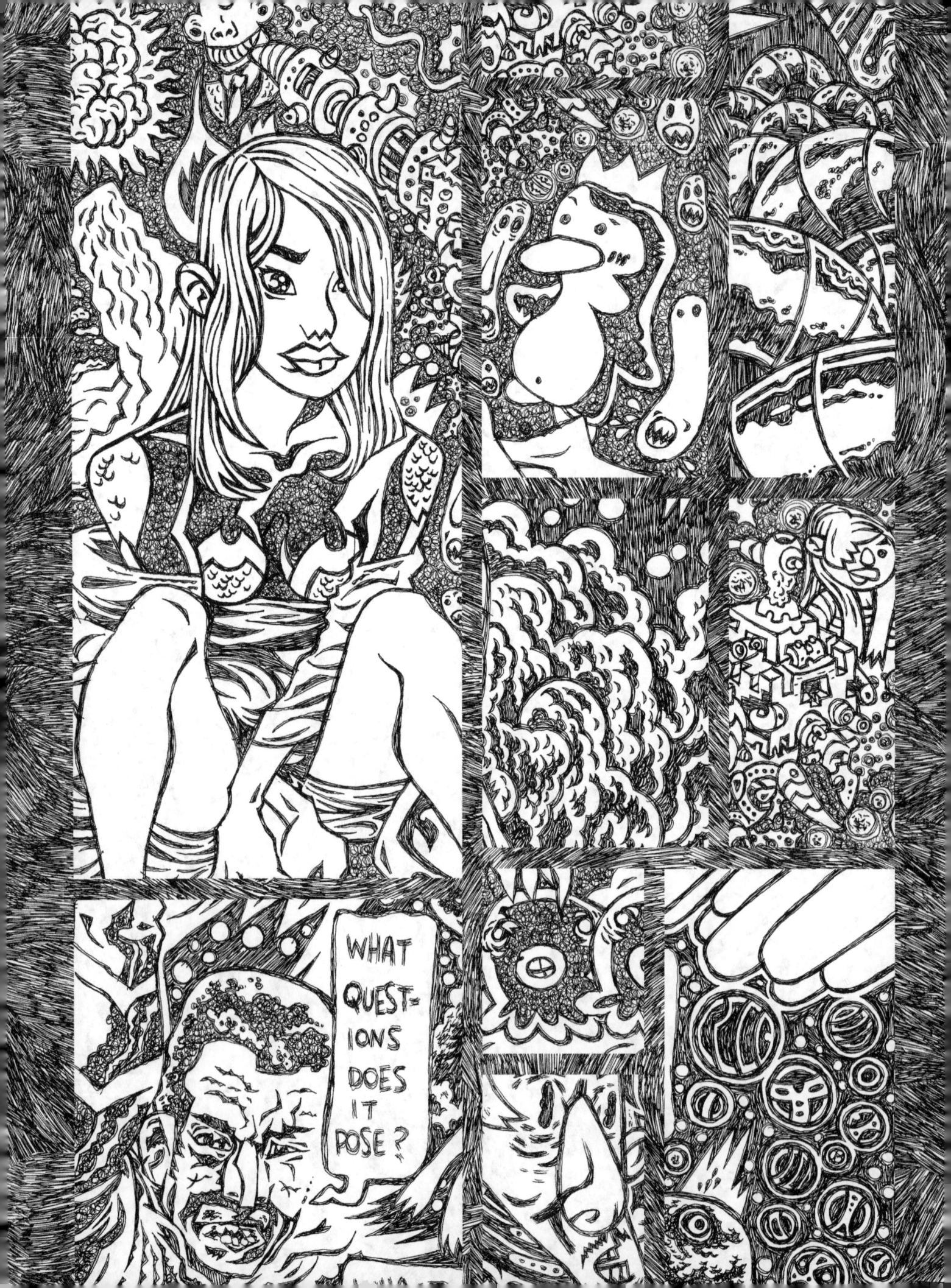

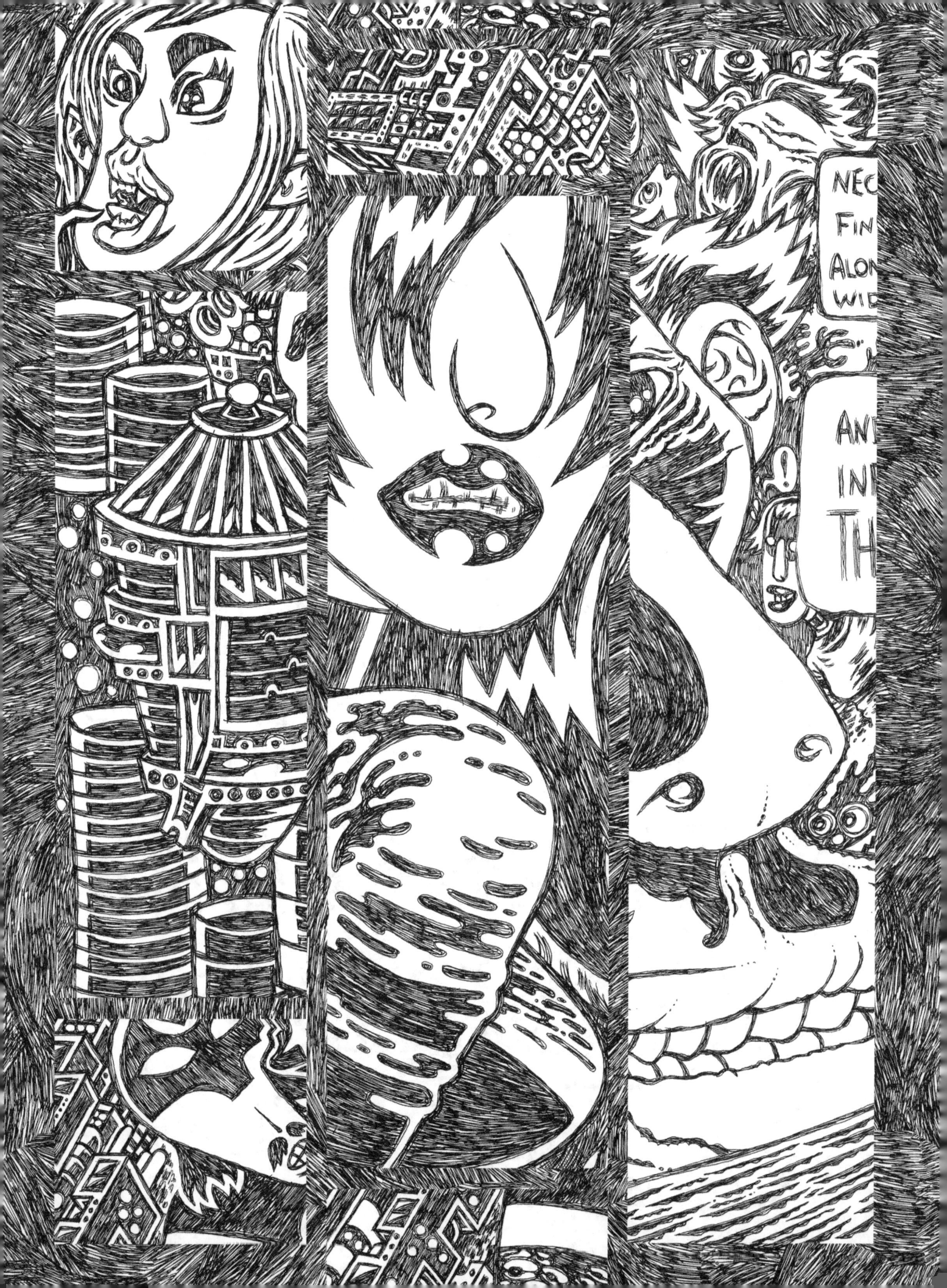

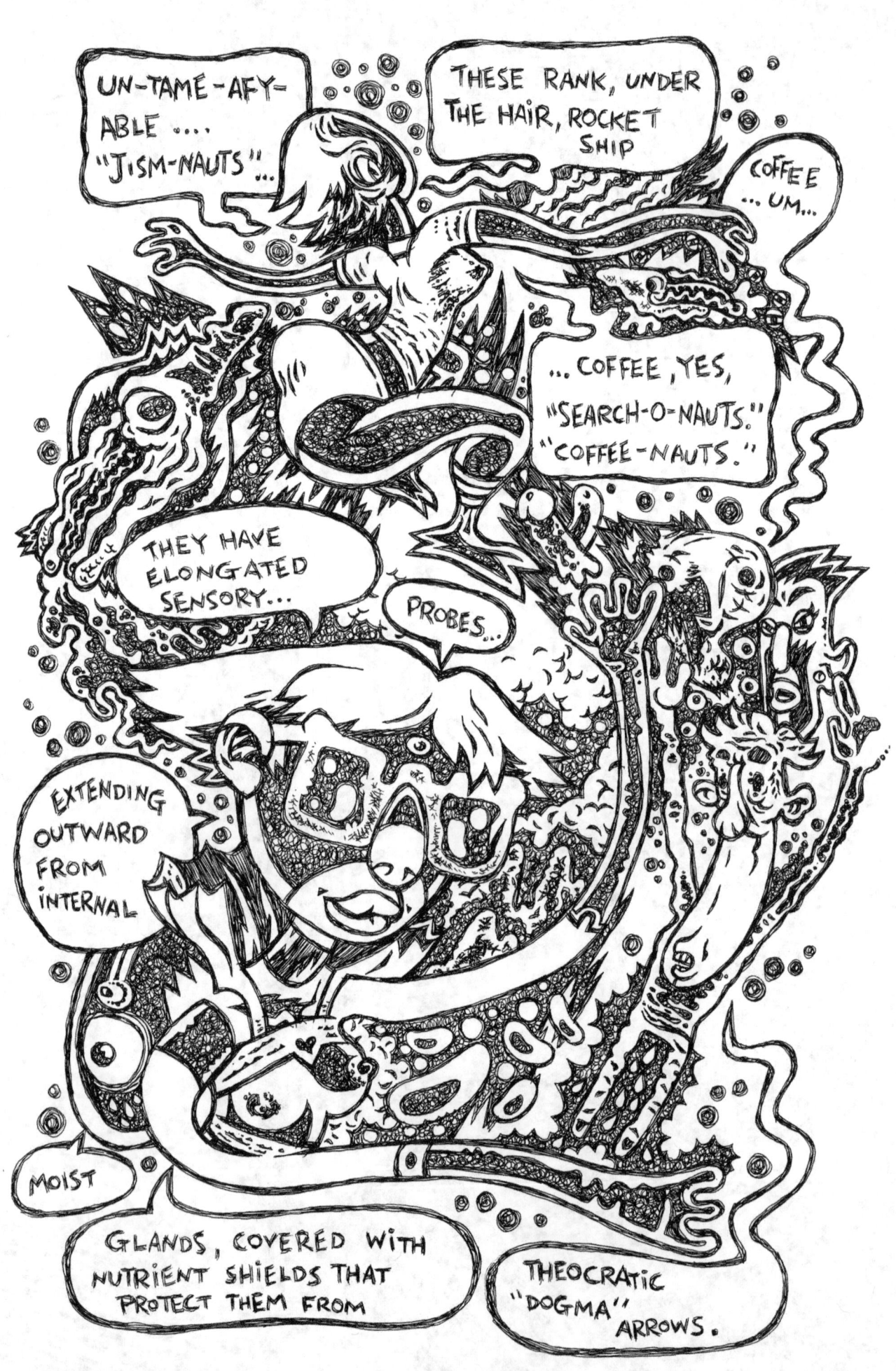

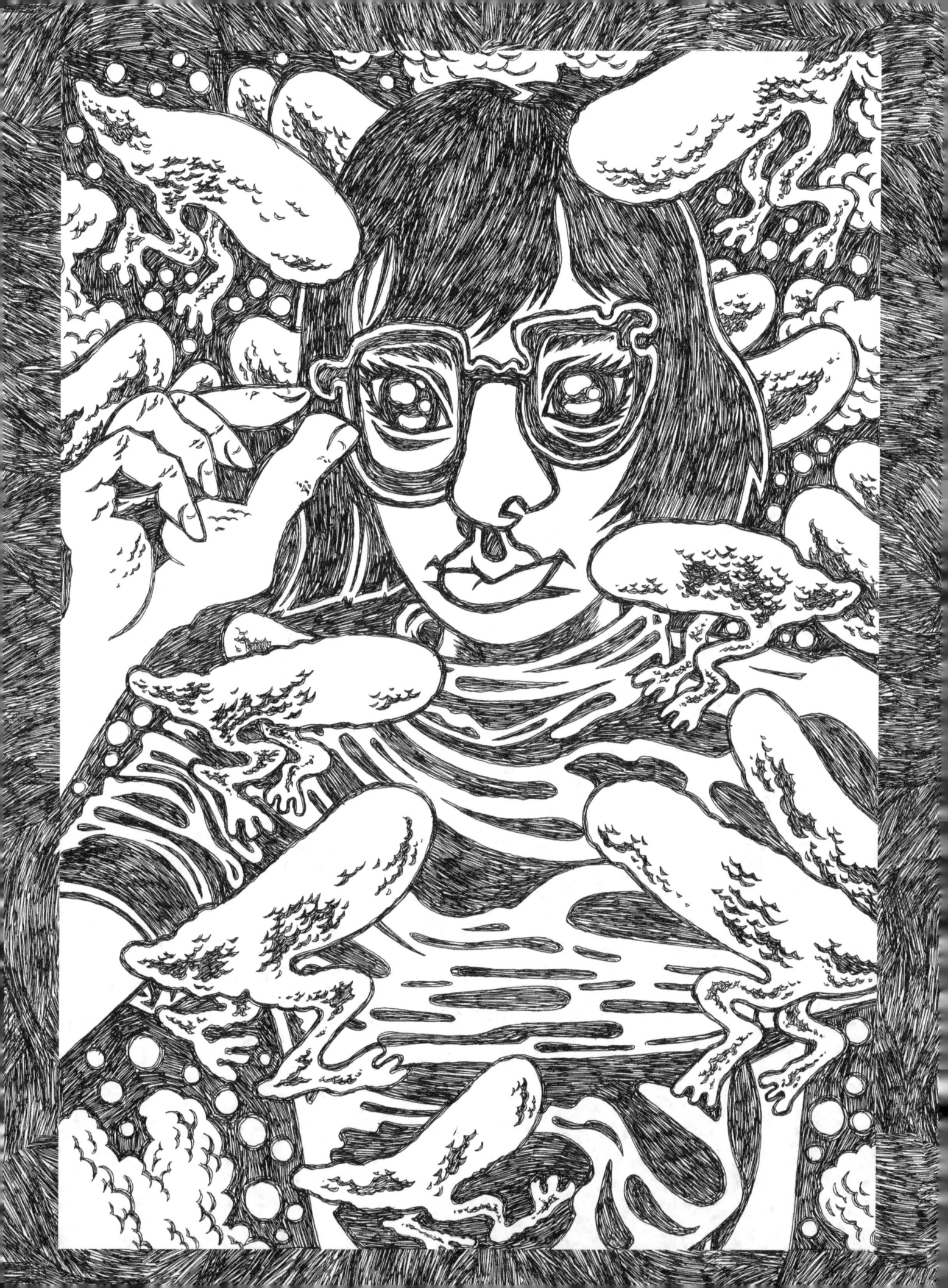

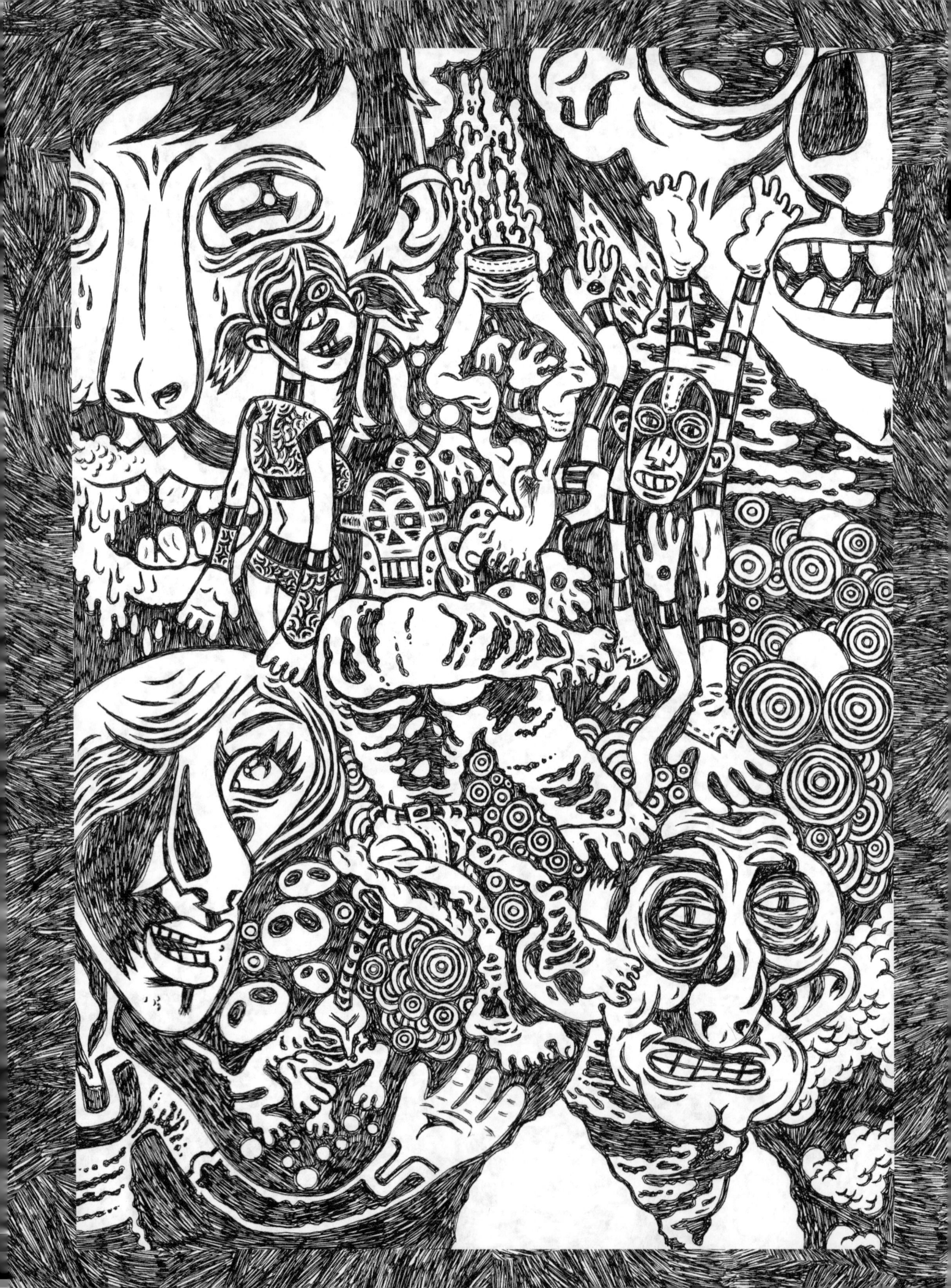

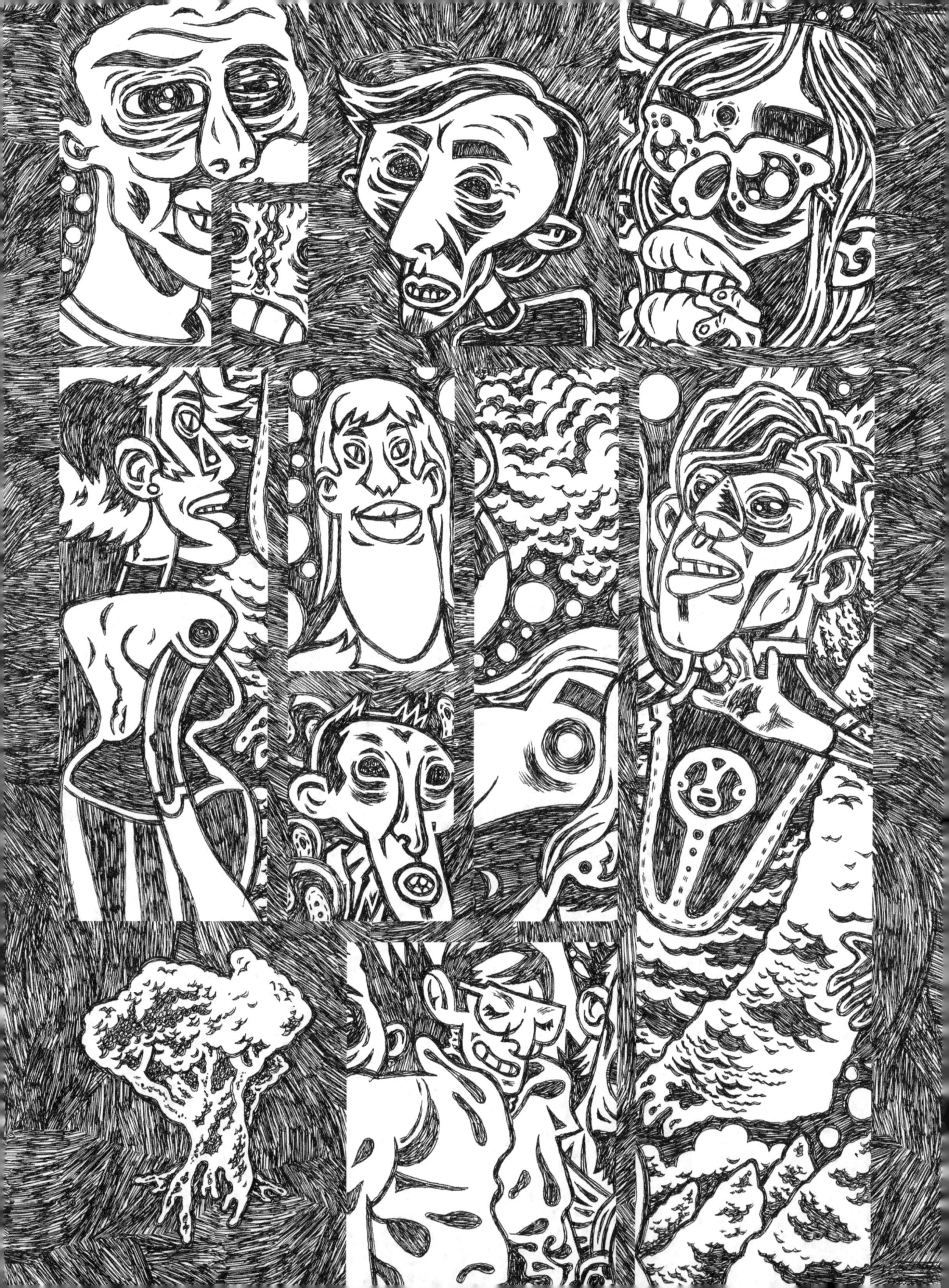

BOOKS BY
BUZZ COLEMAN

A TIGER AGAINST THOUGHT
LIGHTNING JIM
THE FLEXOR AMALGAM
THE SCRATCHY EYE

(AVAILABLE ONLINE AT
AMAZON AND CREATESPACE)

WEBSITE:
DRUIDFLUIDCOMICS.BLOGSPOT.JP

E-MAIL:
FLEXLAMONT@HOTMAIL.CO.JP